MORNING GOD!

PEARL SJÖLANDER

Book Three
GOD AT WORK
IN OUR LIVES

Cover photograph
LUDWIG WERNER BINEMANN
DAVID ASKHAM

Copyright © Dr. Pearl Sjölander
First published 1992

ISBN 1 873796 11 0

Published by Autumn House
a division of The Stanborough
Press, Alma Park, Grantham,
Lincs., NG31 9SL, England

GOOD MORNING GOD!

Readings for Family Worship and School Assemblies.

In this volume — one of three — much-travelled teacher Dr. Pearl Sjölander uses her own adventures and those of others as the basis for morning readings for worship in either home or school.

Dr. Sjölander believes that — whether in the home or at school — worship time should be quality time.

'What is heard in worship — whether at home or at school — is not heard by the world, but it will be heard by posterity.'

VISCOUNT TONYPANDY

THE OPEN FIRE

For you are great and do marvellous deeds; you alone are God.

PSALM 86:10

The flat in which my brother and I grew up was part of a large old house in which nearly every room had an open fire. During the winter, after having been to church, we used to light the fire in the living room and the family would sit around it talking or reading before we went out for an afternoon walk. My brother and I often went out into the woods with some of the other Christian young people who lived nearby. We would walk for hours.

One such afternoon my parents were not home, but my brother Warwick and I lit the fire as usual and sat and enjoyed it while we talked. Then when the sun finally decided to look out from behind the clouds we felt the urge to go for a walk. We thought we would go and see if our friends wanted to come into the woods with us. We pulled the logs in the grate apart so that they would stop burning, put on our warm clothes and set out. It took about fifteen minutes to get to where our friends lived. We had almost gone that far when both Warwick and I began to talk of turning back. We both felt we should do so but had no idea why. We were still keen on going for a walk, so it had nothing to do with tiredness.

We turned and walked home quickly, a feeling of anxiety spurring us on. When we reached home and unlocked the front door we noticed the smell of smoke. We ran into the living room where we had sat round the fire. There on the floor the linoleum had started to burn and a narrow belt of fire was working its way along the lino towards the long curtains which hung down to the floor. In a few more minutes a big fire would have been inevitable. As it was, we soon had things under control.

When the first feeling of fright had gone we just sat there filled with thankfulness to Someone who could see what we couldn't see, and had sent us home in time. Three other families lived in the same big house, so things could have turned out catastrophically.

PRAYER: Thank you, God, for caring about us and protecting us, even when we are not always as careful as we should be.

5

GOD'S MONEY

The Lord . . . will bless those who fear the Lord
— small and great alike.
PSALM 115:12, 13

As soon as he turned the key in the door Mr. Jones felt that something was wrong. He hurriedly opened the door to see what could have happened. To his horror he saw that someone had rummaged through the whole house. Drawers had been pulled out and emptied, in fact the floors looked like battlefields. What had the thief been looking for? Had he found something of value, and if so, what? Mr. Jones knew he had few valuables. He and his family lived a simple life. The little they had saved was kept in the bank. They had never owned any jewellery or other items of value. That is probably why he had never feared that anyone would even try to break into his house — there was nothing worth stealing.

He hadn't been thinking along these lines very long before he remembered with shock that there was a lot of money in the house — money that wasn't his! He rushed from room to room, over the littered floors, to make sure the thief had gone. Then he crept to his secret hiding place. He was the treasurer for the church he belonged to. It was he who counted the offerings after the church services. He then took this money home to keep it safe until he could bank it on Monday morning. It was now Sunday evening. All God's money had been there in the house. Had the thief found it? Mr. Jones hardly dared to look, he was so afraid he would find it had gone.

But then he thought that this was, after all, God's money. Wouldn't God be able to keep it out of the thief's way? He carefully lifted down the little box which lay in a niche above the fireplace. He lifted out the bag in which the money was kept. It didn't seem to have been touched, and felt as full as when he had put it away. Quickly he counted the money. Not a single penny was missing. His joy and relief knew no bounds.

When the rest of the family came home and together with the police had made a thorough search, it was discovered that the thief had taken all the money he had found. Admittedly the amount was small, but he had managed to make a clean sweep of the house. The only money he had missed was God's money. It was just as if he had been prevented from seeing that little niche above the fireplace.

PRAYER: Thank you, Lord, for blessing your people who are part of the work of the church.

DARE TO LET GO

Let us throw off everything that hinders and the sin that so easily entangles, and let us run with perseverance the race marked out for us.
HEBREWS 12:1

Two mountaineers had climbed up a high rock face. It had been slow, hard going, and it required skill and care. The two men were experienced climbers with good equipment. This was fortunate because they were overtaken by a storm before they could reach the top of the rock face and seek safety. All they could do was try to reach a small ledge close by and then tie themselves with their ropes to the rock wall. That way they wouldn't get blown off by the strong winds and fall the several hundred metres down to the next mountain plateau.

The two men had to sit there for several days, chilled through by the rain and snow and the biting winds. If only the weather would lift they could be rescued! They knew that no one could search for them until the weather had stabilized. When at last the clouds lifted and visibility improved and the winds had dropped, a helicopter came to look for them. The pilot was very skilled and used to rescuing people from dangerous situations. When he caught sight of the two men he sent down food, clothing and information on how he would set about rescuing them. It was important, the paper stated, that they obeyed the pilot's orders exactly. Otherwise the helicopter would crash and they would all fall to their deaths.

Weather conditions worsened again and it took a long time before the helicopter could return to pick up the first of the two men. The instructions said that the man was not to grab hold of the lifeline before he had freed himself from the ropes that strapped him to the rock face. His friend held on to him while he untied himself and reached out carefully to grab the rope which was dangling from the helicopter. All went well. Then it was the turn of the second man. This would be much harder as he was alone and had no one to hold him in place on the narrow rock-ledge. He was so stiff with cold that even the simplest movements became clumsy and difficult. Would he dare to untie himself? Would he be able to grab the lifeline without falling to his death? He was afraid but wise enough to follow the instructions, knowing that the life of the pilot also depended on him. As the helicopter hovered over him he untied himself with stiff frozen fingers, his heart beating fast. He carefully lifted his arms to reach the rope, and after several attempts he was finally able to hold it long enough to hook the clip onto his harness and be lifted up to safety.

PRAYER: Lord, you want me to be saved. Lift me to safety and help me to let go of sin.

JOHN WESLEY

"But blessed is the man who trusts in the Lord, whose confidence is in him."
JEREMIAH 17:7

John Wesley was riding from a town where he had been preaching to his next appointment. He soon noticed that he was not the only one on the road. From the side of the road he could at first hear whispers and footsteps. But soon the voices grew louder and angry men shouted at him. He could tell that several of the group were under the influence of alcohol. This didn't surprise John Wesley. Because he preached against the use of alcohol he was often the butt of criticism and derision from drunken mobs.

Now he wondered what was going to happen next. The men who were closing in on him were angry to put it mildly. He was surprised that such a large crowd had been able to gather this far out along the road, and he thought they must have something special in mind. This became evident when the men began to throw stones at John and his horse. Soon clubs were being brandished and John's horse was completely surrounded as the men tried to knock him down. This type of treatment was not new to the pastor, he had been through it all before and survived. Still, there was never any knowing what angry drunken men would do.

It didn't take the crowd long to club John Wesley to the ground. He ended up on his knees, surrounded by men with murder on their minds. He did what he always did, he turned to the Lord. He called out loudly to the only One who could save him. The mob stood back slightly, listening. He was talking loudly, but he didn't seem to be afraid. How strange that someone can trust in an invisible God when he is surrounded by angry men who want to kill him. Without realizing it, the men drew back further and formed a circle round the praying pastor. God seemed to be so real to him. How strange that God can make people so calm when their very life is in danger. Even though they hated John Wesley, a sneaking feeling of respect came over them as they listened to him talking to God.

Suddenly the ringleader stepped forward and put his hand on the praying pastor's shoulder and said to him: 'I will give my life to help you. No one will ever be able to harm you.' The man who said this was George Clifton, the leader of a band of robbers and a professional boxer, a rough, hard man. But from the day George heard John Wesley pray to God as a Friend he became a changed man. He spent the rest of his life doing what Wesley did, travelling round and preaching about Jesus the Saviour.

PRAYER: Help me to trust in you completely in all situations.

THE LIE DETECTOR

Therefore each of you must put off falsehood and speak truthfully to his neighbour.
EPHESIANS 4:25

Two men were accused of the same crime. One of them was guilty, one was innocent. But which was which? Both men denied outright that they had anything to do with the crime, and both of them had very good arguments and explanations as to why they should not be condemned as guilty. The Caliph in the old Muslim state looked at both men for a long time and then called for his servant. He whispered something in the man's ear and the servant left the room. After a while he returned with two bowls with a spoon in each. Both bowls contained dried rice.

The Caliph, who was a very wise man, wanted to judge correctly in this case, so he asked the two accused men to take a large mouthful of rice and chew it for a long time. It was no easy task as the rice was both hard and dry, and the men were not offered any water to drink. The Caliph told them not to swallow what they were chewing. The two men were rather surprised by all this. How strange to have to stand and chew rice in the middle of a court case. But neither of them dared to question the Caliph's orders and they kept chewing.

After some minutes the Caliph told the two men to spit out what they had chewed onto a plate. Surprised, they did what he said. He then stepped down from his throne and took a brief look at the contents of the two plates. Then he went and sat down again. After a short silence he said: 'Now I know who is the guilty one.' He pointed to one of the men who was then taken off to prison. The other man was freed, amazed but relieved.

Those who worked with the Caliph when he sat in judgement knew how the whole thing worked. Both men had chewed and chewed, but the guilty man was very frightened and therefore his mouth was dry. When the rice was spat out the Caliph could see who had a guilty conscience. The rice was still about as dry as when he had started to chew it.

What we do affects our bodies. If we make someone happy we feel happy too and feel better. When we have a bad conscience, or when we lie, it is not just our conscience which is affected, but also our physical body. When we do things that are wrong we don't feel very well either.

PRAYER: Lord, you know I sometimes find it hard to tell the truth. Help me not to lie, even if it is hard to resist.

A SQUASHED FINGER

" 'Whatever you did for one of the least of these brothers of mine, you did for me.' "
MATTHEW 25:40

Sometimes there comes a period when everything seems to go wrong. On one occasion some years ago my husband was away on a trip and I was home alone with our three small sons. This wasn't *too* bad, but just at that time I contracted a severe bout of flu. This made me so weak that I spent most of the time lying on the floor trying to keep an eye on the lively threesome. It was winter with snow and cold winds, so when the 3-year-old opened the outside door I called to him to shut it again immediately. He did as he was told, without looking to see where his 2-year-old brother had his fingers. One finger got caught in the hinge side of the door. When we quickly opened the door again the top part of his third finger hung loose and the blood just ran. I can't stand the sight of blood, and to make matters worse I was weak and dizzy. What was I to do? It was 16km (10 miles) to the nearest hospital and I had no car. We were new to the area and had only got to know one neighbour well. Fortunately he was at home when I phoned, but he had no car either at the time, and had to run to another neighbour to borrow one and drive us to Casualty. There a doctor sewed the top of David's finger back on again.

The thankfulness I felt when the neighbour did all he could to help me when I felt I just couldn't cope any more is beyond description. It was just a simple act, but it meant so much just then. It made me realize how important simple acts of kindness can be to people.

Perhaps you will have the privilege of helping someone today with something big or small. Do it willingly — it means so much to have a helping hand.

PRAYER: May I be of help to someone today. Show me who needs me.

LETTERS

You yourselves are our letter, written on our hearts, known and read by everybody. You show that you are a letter from Christ ... written not with ink but with the Spirit of the living God.
2 CORINTHIANS 3:2, 3

When you get a letter you can see by just looking at it quite a lot about the person who sent it. The letter may have been written in a hurry, untidily, or the writer may have put a lot of effort into making it look beautiful. So without reading any of the words you can still get some insight into what the writer is like. Then once you start reading the letter you find out even more, such as what the writer thinks about different things or people. Perhaps you can learn what hobbies and interests he has. In other words, a letter is not just something you read but also a source of information about the sender.

Occasionally you can come across forged letters. Someone may be writing in someone else's name, perhaps in order to spread lies or slander. It's not nice to receive a letter like that. It makes you sad to be deceived.

It usually means a lot to a person to get a letter. According to today's text a letter is far more important than you would think. Here it says that people who have accepted Jesus become like letters, Christlike letters, who can tell others something about Jesus, the sender. In other words people look at Christians and by watching they form a picture of what God is like. What sort of letters are we? Are we forgeries, pretending to belong to Christ while in actual fact doing many things which are contrary to his ways? This must give the onlooker a very strange picture of God whose 'letter' we are. They may be tempted to think he is a two-faced person, someone they don't want to have anything to do with. Or can people in your daily life catch a glimpse of God's love for them, of his thoughtfulness and goodness? This is how Jesus, the 'letter-writer', would like people to be able to 'read' us.

PRAYER: Help me today to give a correct picture of you by what I do and say, so that I can be a genuine Christlike letter.

THE ART OF COMMUNICATING

"But when he, the Spirit of truth, comes, he will guide you into all truth. He will not speak on his own; he will speak only what he hears, and he will tell you what is yet to come."
JOHN 16:13

Nowadays people have many different ways of communicating with each other. There's the telephone, satellite TV, short-wave radio and computers. People can reach each other over vast distances, even from out in space, and it all happens so quickly.

Before all these communication systems came to the aid of man there were many other ways of sending messages. If you were out at sea and wanted to send a message to another ship which had come within sight you used a system of signal flags called semaphore. It is still used today. You signal with the flags in each hand, and spell out words by holding the flags in different positions. The letter R is made by holding both hands straight out from the body so that the flags are horizontal. Letter D is signalled by one flag held above the head while the other is right down by the knee.

If you wanted to send messages that were to be heard, as opposed to semaphoring which had to be seen, you could use Morse code with its system of dots and dashes, or long and short sounds. If you wanted to call for help using Morse code, the way to signal SOS was, and still is, three short, three long and three short sounds, or dots and dashes. You can use Morse even without an electric transmitter, for example, by flashing long and short intervals with a torch on a dark night. Even smoke signals can be made into Morse messages, but that is quite a slow process.

In West Africa I both saw and heard another system of sending messages from village to village. Drums were used which tried to imitate the human voice and human speech-patterns and rhythms. These were called the talking drums and they could be heard clearly over long distances. The villagers could not only hear but also understand what was being said by the drums far in the jungle.

On one of the Canary Islands called Goera, the locals have an unusual way of communicating when they need to send messages from one high mountain ridge to another. They use a whistling language. Whistling carries well over the deep mountain valleys. Those who are really good at this language can make themselves heard up to a distance of 6-10km. Children on the island grow up bilingual. They speak Spanish and have a well-developed whistling language too. This latter is quite detailed and can be used for sending very exact messages. If someone falls ill way up in a mountain village the message, with the details, is whistled from village to village along the many mountain ridges till the message reaches the capital San Sebastian, where the doctor lives. He will then know where to go and what condition he is to treat.

PRAYER: Thank you, Lord, that you have many ways of speaking to my heart. Help me to listen to what you have to say through your Holy Spirit.

GOD HAS STRANGE HELPERS

Then the word of the Lord came to Elijah: " . . . and hide in the ravine of Kerith . . . . You will drink from the brook, and I have ordered the ravens to feed you there."
1 KINGS 17:2-4

She lived alone in a little old house way out in the woods. It was her parental home. She had always lived there and had looked after the smallholding and survived on what she could grow and on the few chickens she kept. But now she was old and the only one left in the family. She wasn't unhappy about being alone or living in such isolation. It was nice to be able to do just what she wanted, when she wanted.

Summer and autumn had come and gone. Now the long, cold, hard winter was back. She had always lived here in the north of Finland so she was used to the dark months and the large amounts of snow. But now she was a little anxious. The winter was at its coldest and the snow reached up to the window sills. None of her distant neighbours had visited her for several months. They were also getting old and tired. She wouldn't even have thought about this if it hadn't been for the fact that she had begun to feel so unusually weak and tired herself.

Soon she was feeling so ill that she could no longer make her way in the snow the many miles to get help. The food was almost finished. Was she going to have to starve to death? She turned to God and asked him for help. She wondered how and when God would answer her prayer.

Some hours later she felt impressed to open the front door. She made her way slowly towards it and found in the snow on her porch a few small fishes. She picked them up with a thankful heart and looked to see if there were footprints in the snow. There were none to be seen. Full of wonderment she took the fishes into the kitchen and cooked them. The following day there were more fishes outside her door! How had they arrived there? She was determined to find out. The next day she made herself comfortable in a chair by the window which overlooked the porch. She was going to keep watching till she found out how the fishes came there. Finally she saw something dark moving across the white snow. When it drew closer she could see that it was a dog. It came up to her door, put down a few fishes, turned and disappeared into the woods.

The dog continued to come with fish every day until the little old lady was feeling better and the snow had begun to melt. Then she could go out again and manage on her own. She never saw the dog again and never found out who it belonged to. None of her far-flung neighbours had a dog like that.

PRAYER: Thank you for all the ways you have of looking after us, you who are Lord of the animals too.

PIANO PUPILS

**For it is not those who hear the law who are righteous
in God's sight, but it is those who obey the law who will be
declared righteous.**
ROMANS 2:13

My piano pupils come to me once a week. I listen to the pieces
I have set them for homework the week before, and then we discuss various aspects of the new pieces I set them for the coming
week. It is my job as a teacher to try by all means to inspire
my pupils to want to practise faithfully during the week. It is only
by practising that they can make any progress. It doesn't matter
how good a teacher I am, or how well I can explain the technical
details, if the pupils don't put what I say into practice during the
week they won't improve as pianists.

Many Christians seem to think that they can make spiritual progress merely by going to the 'lessons', that is to say, going to church
once a week. Between each visit to the church they in no way
put into practice what they learn there. They think they can learn
all about the Christian way of life merely by hearing someone
explain about the hows and whys.

God wants us to build up a personal relationship with him and
learn to know him personally, every day of the week. He wants
to teach us through our own experiences to trust his promises,
to hold on when things get tough, to choose to do the right when
faced with alternatives. Your pastor perhaps says: 'God can help
you to stand up to temptations.' It is not enough for you just to
know this theoretically. You have to pray for God's help every
day, and for the strength you need to stand up to the temptations
you meet. In that way you are practising what you have learned
and you can grow spiritually and experience God's power to save
you. God is no longer a Friend you meet once a week in church
but Someone who goes with you wherever you are.

*PRAYER: Help me every day to put into practice what I have learned
about the Christian life so that I can grow spiritually.*

THE PASTOR'S HANDS

**The arm of the Lord is not too short to save, nor his
ear too dull to hear.**
ISAIAH 59:1

I was about 9 years old when an Australian pastor visited our home.
He was very pleasant but he certainly looked 'different'. He had
large scars on his hands and on his kind face. It wasn't long

before I just had to ask him how he came to be so injured. This is what he told me.

Back home in Australia he had had a series of meetings in a small church hall. People came back week after week to hear more about the Bible and about Jesus. One day the pastor decided to show his congregation a Bible film. Everyone was watching it with interest when the projector suddenly caught fire. The pastor, who was standing right next to it, had his face badly burnt. With his hands he tried to stifle the flames but the fire spread quickly. The projector stood at the back of the hall, near the doors, so it was impossible to get out that way. The pastor and his assistant managed to open a window at the other end of the hall and started to lift the panic-stricken people to safety.

There were many people in the hall and it took a long time to get them all out. As they worked the flames came closer. The heat became almost unbearable and the smoke made them feel sick, but there was no time to think about things like that. It was a matter of saving lives. The pastor kept praying all the time that his severe burns and the terrible pain he felt in his hands every time he helped someone through the window wouldn't make him pass out. He so desperately wanted to save all those who had come to the meeting. When the last of the people had been lifted out the flames were so close that the two men thought they would catch fire any minute.

Completely exhausted and weak from the awful pain, Pastor Rudge thought he was going to collapse. His strength was completely gone and the pain in his face and hands kept on increasing. Now he was conscious only of the great pain. He could hardly think logically any more. The window was too high for the two exhausted men to climb out without help. Just when they thought their last moment had come they felt a big strong hand lift them up and out through the window, and before they could grasp what was happening they found themselves outside the blazing church.

PRAYER: Thank you, Lord, for having the power to save us from both danger and temptation. Be with me today.

DESMOND DOSS
Be strong in the Lord and in his mighty power.
EPHESIANS 6:10

Desmond Doss was a medical orderly. There was nothing outstanding about him, though his friends might have thought him a little strange. He read his Bible and prayed every day. Desmond was an American, and the time we are talking about was during 15 the Second World War. Desmond didn't work in an ordinary hospital in his homeland. Instead he was a medical orderly who took care of wounded Americans from the battlefields around the Pacific. No cushy job, but of vital importance for the injured.

One day a unit of American troops had made their way up a very steep mountain by the aid of a rope ladder. The idea was to attack the enemy from this high plateau. Desmond had gone along in case anyone was injured. Here at Okinawa one of the bloodiest battles of the Second World War was being fought. The platoon from the American 77th division was forced to retreat — and with speed. But how could this be accomplished speedily when everyone had to go down one rope ladder?

Fifty-five men managed to get down over the cliff face by means of the ladder. Left up on the plateau were 100 injured and dying men, plus Desmond Doss. His commander ordered him to come down. The bombardment of the cliff top was now too intense for anyone to survive there. But Desmond refused to come down. Soon the group at the foot of the rope ladder could see what he was doing. He was tying an injured soldier with a rope and slowly lowering him down to shelter and help. But Desmond was not content to help *one* man from certain death. Under continuous fire from the enemy he carefully made his way from one injured soldier to the other. He dragged and carried them one at a time to the cliff edge and lowered them to safety, a heavy and very dangerous task. Some of the soldiers had already died from their wounds but the rest, seventy-five men in all, were rescued by Desmond working there all alone. Every second he was in grave danger, the firing continuing unabated all the while. But he felt he couldn't desert the wounded who were under his care. Not until all the seventy-five were safely down did he climb down the rope ladder himself.

Later he was given America's highest award for bravery. When someone asked him how he had been able to be so brave he answered: 'I am not at all a brave person, but when I prayed to God he took away my fear. God gave me the courage.'

PRAYER: Help me to turn to you when I need courage or strength. Thank you for being willing and able to give the strength needed to manage all the difficulties I may meet.

GIVING OF ONE'S BEST

Let us not love with words or tongue but with actions.

1 JOHN 3:18

It happened on the night of 31 January 1953. A spring tide had caused the level of the sea along the Dutch coast to be about 5 metres higher than usual. When you live in a low-lying country like Holland, where the sea water is held back in many places merely by dam walls or sea defence works, such a rise in the water level is very serious. The danger was worsened by the fact that there had been a storm out at sea to the north and that an almost 1,000-metre-long wall of water had been piled up by the winds. And this wall of water was heading for Holland at the same time as the country was threatened by a spring flood. The result was that the sea level rose until it poured over the protective walls and dykes and spread itself out over large parts of Holland. Thousands of people lost all they owned.

Those who lived on slightly higher ground opened their homes for these homeless people. Mass accommodation was also arranged where possible. It was a matter of getting a roof over their heads and at least some warmth so that the poor, wet people wouldn't succumb to disease in the midwinter cold. Then came the matter of finding clothes, household utensils, furniture, etc. It was like starting from scratch again.

Henney lived in a village to which people had come to find help and shelter. She was only 9 years old and rather shy. Near her home people had turned a warehouse into temporary accommodation for a large number of the homeless. Her mother asked her to come along to the place to see if they could be of some help. Henney and her family had all they needed and more. They were in a position to give away clothes and other things. Mother felt strongly that they should share their belongings with others. So Henney went up to her room and picked out some winter clothes that were too small for her and put them in a bag.

When they got to the warehouse where the still-shocked people were housed, Henney had a lump in her throat. It hurt her to see children her own age frightened and sad. She wished she could do something for at least one of them. Now she saw these children with her own eyes she was no longer content to give them just her cast-offs. She sneaked out of the big door, ran home, and looked in her wardrobe once more. She was no longer unsure of what she wanted to do. She picked out her newest and warmest jumper, her favourite, the one which had given her so much pleasure to receive. That was the one she 17 wanted to give away in the hope that someone else would be made happy by receiving it.

PRAYER: Help me to show in my actions that I love my fellow men. Make me willing to give of my best.

IN THE SNOW

For a man's ways are in full view of the Lord, and he examines all his paths.
PROVERBS 5:21

Today's story took place many years ago out in the Swedish countryside. In a little home out in the woods lived a mother with her three small children. Their father was having to work in another area. The baby had become ill, and the food was running out. The mother felt she couldn't leave her sick baby while she walked the long distance to the nearest shop, so when the food had gone she decided she must send the two older children. They had been offering to go for several days but their mother was anxious because the journey was long and the snow was deep and it was very cold. But now she had no alternative and the two, about 8 and 9 years old, set off, promising not to sit down in the snow however tired they became.

They arrived at the shop all right. But getting back home was more difficult. The shopping basking was heavy and the two children were tired. The younger one cried quietly as she plodded slowly on in the deep snow along the unmarked path through the woods. Each step she took in the snow made her more tired. In the end she just couldn't manage any more and cried so loudly that her bigger brother, who was also exhausted, agreed that they should sit down and rest for a short while. What their mother had been so afraid of had happened. The two tired children fell asleep and were soon covered by the snow which had started to fall again.

A farmer was on his way home from the village with his horse and sleigh, but today something seemed to be wrong with his horse. It had stopped suddenly, without any reason. The farmer called out, used his whip, but the horse stayed put. The farmer went up to his horse, talked to it and tried to pull it by its bridle to get it going again. Nothing happened. Given that his horse was usually very obedient the farmer thought that maybe it was aware of some danger he couldn't see. He had heard others talk about animals' instincts. So he unfastened the horse from the sleigh to see what it would do.

18   To his surprise the horse began to retrace its steps. After a while

it stopped and began to paw the soft snow by the wayside. The farmer ran up to see what it could be and saw a patch of red material. Then he began to dig in the snow and found the two sleeping children.

He wrapped them in his furs and drove them home as fast as he could. He knew them well. The waiting mother had been praying for her two children all the time they had been away.

PRAYER: It is good to know that you see everything, dear Lord, and can save us from all kinds of difficulties and dangers.

SAINT BARTHOLOMEW'S

When you make a vow to God, do not delay in fulfilling it. . . . It is better not to vow than to make a vow and not fulfil it.
ECCLESIASTES 5:4, 5

Rahere was visiting Rome when he suddenly fell ill. Very ill. At that time, the beginning of the twelfth century, there was not much medical help to be had. Rahere was afraid he was going to die and therefore, like so many others in similar situations, he called on God for help. He promised God that if he recovered he would show his gratitude by helping others who were ill. With time Rahere was restored to health and he spent considerable time thinking over the promise he had made to God. What was he to do in order to keep it?

One night he had a dream. In the dream he seemed to be instructed to return to London where he had earlier worked as jester at the court of Henry I. Once back at court he was to ask the king for a plot of ground called 'Smooth-field'. The Lord would help him with the rest of the project. Rahere took his dream seriously. However, when he returned to the palace the whole court made fun of him. A jester who had gone serious — what a joke! Rahere was determined, however. When given an audience with the king he requested that Smooth-field be given to him. Everyone thought he must be mad. What on earth was he going to do with that stinking swampy area? Of course he could have it — no one else had any use for it!

Rahere didn't know how to start now that he had the land. No one wanted to listen to his idea, let alone give him a hand to help it materialize. However, it wasn't long before this small, modest man had won the hearts of the children, children who lived close by Smooth-field. They began to help him collect stones. Before long their parents were also giving a hand. To all who came Rahere explained his simple plan and it soon seemed as though half of London had heard of it. People began to donate money and materials which were needed for the building. Gradually, 19 on that previously swampy ground, a little church and a hospital were erected. Rahere called the place St. Bartholomew's.

The hospital was very simple, but it was clean, and everyone who worked there was kind, even to the poor — an unusual thing in those days. So many sick made their way there that it wasn't long before the hospital had to be extended. Rahere died in 1140. He had kept his promise to God. He had helped the sick. There is still a hospital on that spot today, and it still has the same name. Now it's a large, famous hospital. And it all began with a court jester who made God a promise and then kept it.

PRAYER: Lord, help me to keep the promises I make to you and to others.

DAD AND I

Jesus answered: . . . "Anyone who has seen me has seen the Father."
JOHN 14:9

My father and I are alike in many ways. Just by looking at the two of us you can see that we belong to the same family. I've got the same nose as Dad, and the same brown eyes. My hands are also very much like Dad's. But I am like my father in other ways too.

You see, Dad and I have the same interests. We both like to paint pictures and to look at pictures painted by others. We both like to play the piano, to sing and to listen to music, even the same sort of music. We have both had the same education and are both language teachers. We laugh at the same type of jokes and think alike on many subjects. But this is not the same thing as being a copy of my father. We are two very different people who happen to have quite a few things in common.

Jesus was with his disciples for a relatively short period of time. About three years. It took them a long time to work out how Jesus and God, his Father, related to each other. It took them time even to progress as far as believing he was the Son of God. But once they had that clear they longed to meet Jesus' Father, to see him for themselves. That was their greatest wish. Jesus answered them with the words in today's text. What he was saying was, 'I am like my father, I do his will, and I carry out his actions and live and behave just as God does. You have seen God when you have seen me.' In other words, Jesus was so like his Father that he could go so far as to say that the two of them were one. So alike were they when it came to what they wanted to do for the world and for mankind.

I am like my father. Those who meet me receive some idea

of what Dad is like. I have also chosen to have God as my heavenly Father. I sometimes wonder how like him I have become. Do I live in such a way that people who see me and hear me think that God must be my Father? It would be wonderful if that was the case.

PRAYER: Heavenly Father, come into my heart and live in me so that I can show others how wonderful and loving you are.

A LOAD OFF HIS MIND

He who conceals his sins does not prosper, but whoever confesses and renounces them finds mercy.
PROVERBS 28:13

One of the scouts in my group, who often popped in to see me, came over one day looking very serious. This talkative 12-year-old was silent for once. After some gentle prodding it came out. He had a bad conscience. He had had it for quite some time, he said. But after the sermon he had heard in church at the weekend he had realized he ought to do something about his bad conscience. He explained to me that during recent months he had gone in for shop-lifting. On a small scale, admittedly, but still shop-lifting. From the shops around the village square he had taken things like sweets, golf balls, rubbers, trinkets, etc. The previous day he had spent considerable time working out what all these things had cost and how much he owed each shopkeeper. Seventy-five pence here, £1.50 there, and so on. He had also counted out his savings into piles of the right amount. Everything was ready, and only the most difficult part remained to be done.

Today he was going to go to each of the shops, tell them what he had done, apologize and hand over the money. He had to do this, he said, because he felt he couldn't live with his bad conscience a moment longer. But he was very nervous, and asked me if I would come along with him and wait for him outside the shops.

The lad went bravely into one shop after the other. Sometimes he was in there a long time. Sometimes he looked happy when he came back out, sometimes hurt and sad. Apparently some of the shop owners had cross-examined him and scolded him, while others had been kind and understanding.

When everything was put right we cycled back to my house and drank some juice while he told me what had happened in the various shops. Despite the unkind remarks he had still had the courage to continue to the next shop. I really admired him. I hadn't realized he had it in him. Nor had *he*, apparently. As he rose 21 to leave he said something I shall never forget: 'This has been the hardest thing I've ever done, but it was worth it. It is so wonderful to have a clear conscience again at last!'

PRAYER: Lord, give me courage enough to go and put things right when I have done wrong. Help me to be really sorry for what I have done.

THE GROUP

But the Lord is faithful, and he will strengthen and protect you from the evil one.
2 THESSALONIANS 3:3

Very few of us like to be the odd ones out — not part of the crowd. As a Christian it does happen sometimes that you feel a little like an outsider. Perhaps you are the only one in your circle of acquaintances who believes in God. To be the odd one out in such a group is not easy. Groups of friends tend to put special demands on their members which may cause problems for Christians. To what extent should a Christian be willing to compromise in order to be popular and to be 'one of the gang'? Should he or she be willing to start swearing, telling dirty jokes, take part in pilfering, dress in a provocative way, just for the sake of being allowed to be one of the group?

Some Christian young people argue like this. I will do what the group wants in the beginning just to become part of it and make friends. Later on I shall try to witness to the group. This is a dangerous way of arguing for several reasons. First of all, these so-called 'friends' are going to have a hard job understanding what you mean by talking about right and wrong when they know that you have been willing to compromise. No one is going to believe you or be influenced for good by you when you say one thing and do another. Secondly, you can never be sure that once you have become a real part of the group you will be strong enough to stop doing what they want you to do. Peer pressure is very hard to withstand.

The best rule of thumb is to try *not* to pattern your life on those who do what is wrong. You cannot buy real friendship that way. Instead choose to be honest, upright and friendly to everyone you meet. Then you will gradually notice that they will respect and like you for being what you are — your true Christian self.

PRAYER: Lord, give me the strength to withstand the pressure from those who want me to do wrong, and give me the wisdom to see that you are the best Friend anyone can have.

IN THE LAST MINUTE

**"He reached down from on high and took hold of me;
he drew me out of deep waters."**
2 SAMUEL 22:17

Everyone was asleep, rolled up in their sleeping bags. All except the leader of the group, Ernest Shackleton. He was responsible for the twenty-seven men who lay out there in their tents on the ice of Antarctica. He had woken up and felt a vague but strong anxiety. The year was 1915. He dressed quickly and crept out of his tent. It was 11pm. Shackleton and his men had pitched camp on a large ice-floe. He noticed that the floe was no longer as safe as when they had pitched camp. The movement of the water had increased markedly. He realized that the ice-floe they were lying on wouldn't hold much longer. There was an immediate risk that the water would break the floe into smaller pieces.

Before he had finished thinking this thought he heard the low dull sound of cracking ice. Their ice-floe had divided into two and the crack went just where Shackleton was standing and right underneath the tent in which eight of his men lay sleeping. The two parts of the ice-floe began to pull apart, the tent collapsed on the eight men and ended up in the icy water. Seven of them quickly fought their way out of the tent and were pulled up onto the ice. Shackleton tugged and pulled at the tent to try to get hold of the eighth man. He could hear that there was someone left in there. In the end he got the tent away and a strange shape was visible in the dark water. There was the eighth man still in his sleeping bag. Shackleton grabbed hold of him and succeeded in getting the thoroughly soaked man up on the ice again.

A few seconds later the two parts of the floe were driven together again with a loud bang which shook them all. If this had happened just a few moments earlier the man in the water would have been crushed to death. But the danger was not over yet. Now it was vital that the man who had been soaked through was kept alive. It was many degrees below freezing and there were no dry clothes for him. In the biting Antarctic wind a man with wet clothes would soon freeze to death.

But his friends fought to keep him alive. They took turns walking backwards and forward on the ice-floe with him all night to keep up his body heat. It worked — he made it.

PRAYER: Thank you for fellow men who are willing to help us when we need it most. Thank you for being even closer to us and even more willing to pull us out of difficulty.

A CHANGED MAN

**"In everything I did, I showed you that . . . we must help the
weak, remembering the words the Lord Jesus himself said:
'It is more blessed to give than to receive.' "**
ACTS 20:35

During the Second World War the Royal Air Force had certain
units which were trained to carry out very demanding jobs. One
such unit, 633 Squadron, were later known as the Dambusters.
One of their most skilled pilots, a man who could drop bombs
exactly on target from very great heights, was called Leonard
Cheshire.

When the war was over Cheshire was strongly impressed to
believe that God existed. Not only that he existed, but also that
he wanted to live in his heart. The pilot gave himself completely
to the Lord. He soon noticed that he was no longer completely
satisfied with his earlier way of life. He was under the growing
conviction that God had some special task for him to perform.
But what could this task be? He didn't know, but spent a lot of
time wondering how he could find out what God had in mind
for him.

Just as he was intent on thinking and praying about his mission
as a Christian he heard, by chance, about an old man who was
all alone and dying of cancer. Feeling that here was something
he could do, Cheshire took the old man into his home. He cared
for him tenderly and lovingly, making the dying man's last days
as bright as possible.

Now the pilot knew what he was going to do with his life.
He would live out his love to God by giving all his time and energy
to people who had no one to look after them, people who were
very ill or severely handicapped. The Lord showed him there were
many people like that. So many, in fact, that he was unable to
take care of them all himself and started looking around for helpers.
After a time this led to the opening of Cheshire Homes all over
England. There are now seventy-seven Cheshire Homes in Britain
and a further 147 in forty-five countries worldwide. These homes
are for people who, for some reason or other, have no relatives
or friends to look after them during serious illness. In Cheshire
Homes they still do today what the RAF pilot who started it all
did — they show gentleness and empathy for those no one else
is able to help.

*PRAYER: Lord show me my mission in life. Show me today someone
whom I can help and support.*

ROBOTS

"Choose for yourselves this day whom you will serve . . . . But as for me and my household, we will serve the Lord."
JOSHUA 24:15

Nowadays there are robots which can do the most amazing things. Some are programmed to speak clearly enough to make themselves understood. Some can hear and 'understand' at least simple messages and answer questions put to them. Other robots can, with the help of batteries, move freely round the room, while others are programmed to move in certain patterns to carry out complicated work operations. A lot of effort is being put into making robots as much like human beings as possible. This is not science fiction but fact.

Particular attention is given to developing better and better 'brains' for robots, so that they can perform more complex tasks. Some are made to carry out precision work and with the aid of a bigger 'memory' can be programmed to carry out many difficult operations in a row. Nowadays robots are so developed that they can be fed with more and more information, enabling them to 'think out' alternatives, make decisions and choices, rather than act automatically. There is also interest in making a robot which can repair itself as the human body does.

Most of the robots in this country are to be found in factories where they are used, among other things, for collecting, putting together, lifting, fastening and correcting. These robots often do the heavy lifting jobs, the dull repetitive jobs or those demanding great precision. You can see robots painting, welding, tightening nuts and bolts — almost anything.

For some time now the robot principles have been used in the construction of weapons. There are now weapons which can reach their destination without anyone steering them — they can steer themselves. There are missiles which can navigate by the aid of the stars, or which are programmed to read off the terrain under them. Others are guided by remote control, or by seeking engine heat. There seems to be no limit to what man can get machines to do. And these machines, these robots, obey blindly and exactly.

God has made us very differently. He could have created us always to do what he wants. He chose instead to give us a free will. He wants us to serve him because we want to and because we love him, not because we are forced to.

PRAYER: Lord, I choose to serve you today. Lead me in everything I do, so that I do what is right and according to your will.

OUT ON THE ICE

How great is your goodness, which you have stored up for those who fear you, which you bestow in the sight of men on those who take refuge in you.
PSALM 31:19.

As the crow flies, Martha and her friend lived quite close to each other. They lived on either side of a bay in Sweden, and were forced to travel into town and then out again in order to get to each other. But it was worth the effort, because there were not many other Christian young people in the area. Besides, they had so much fun, and got on so well.

As Martha and her friend lived in the north of Sweden they had no problems exchanging visits during the winter months. As soon as the bay had frozen over it was just a matter of walking across, or even cycling along the track that nearly everyone used. One afternoon Martha's friend had come across the ice to spend some hours with her. They had had such a lovely time, and now that it was evening she had to return home. Martha decided to walk with her friend across the ice in order to get some fresh air and spin out their time together. Her friend phoned home to say that she was on her way. It was very dark outside and she didn't want her mother to worry.

The two teenagers set off across the bay, talking and laughing, and having a wonderful time all alone out on the ice. Meanwhile, a church member had popped in to visit the mother of Martha's friend. He just happened to ask where her daughter was and the mother explained that she had just phoned and would soon be home because she was coming across the ice. The man became alarmed. He explained that he had just cycled across the ice of the bay and seen that the local ice-breaker was busy making a channel through the ice exactly where he had been cycling. He ran out of the house and set off on his bike as fast as he could to the place where he knew the channel cut across the footpath on the ice. He prayed all the while that he would get there before the girls arrived, so that he could warn them. Reaching the edge of the newly-made channel he could hear the two girls laughing and talking just a few metres away on the other side of the channel which had now become open water for boats to pass along. In the darkness all he could do was call loudly, trying to attract their attention. They heard him and stopped just a metre or two from the edge of the channel. It was barely visible because the broken ice still looked almost as white as the ice on which they were walking. How thankful all three of them were! There was no one else out there on the ice that evening. If the girls had fallen into the channel there would have no one around to help them out of the freezing water among the blocks of ice.

PRAYER: Thank you for your goodness and watchcare in small details as well as matters of life and death.

PYRAMIDS

You are ... members of God's household, built on the foundation of the apostles and prophets, with Christ Jesus himself as the chief corner-stone. In him the whole building is joined together and rises to become a holy temple in the Lord. And in him you too are being built together to become a dwelling in which God lives by his Spirit.
EPHESIANS 2:19-22

There are people who have put a lot of time and energy into building something gigantic, impressive and lasting. The Egyptian pharaohs, for example, had enormous pyramids built, pyramids we can look at today, 4,500 years later. These pyramids were reckoned among the seven wonders of the world. If you have only seen pictures of the pyramids it may be hard to imagine how big they are. The highest is 146 metres high, comparable to a thirty-storey building. Each of the sides of the pyramid is about 230 metres long. These large pyramids cover over 52,609 square metres at their base. They have to be seen to be believed.

In order to construct one such large pyramid about 254,851 cubic metres of large stone blocks were needed. Not easy-to-handle bricks. For example, the Great Pyramid of Khufu is made of smoothly chiselled granite blocks weighing about 2½ tonnes apiece. The completed pyramid consisted of 2,300,000 such granite blocks! Bear in mind, too, that these pyramids were built before the invention of machinery for lifting heavy loads. It must have taken some doing to get those last blocks in place, 146 metres up in the air. The whole process becomes even more amazing when you take into consideration the fact that these granite blocks were not quarried on site but had to be transported over long distances. The largest blocks used in the centre of the pyramids were quarried in Aswan, 1,000km south of where the pyramids stand near Cairo. The smaller limestone blocks which make up the outer layer of the pyramid's surface were quarried in Turan, on the other side of the River Nile.

Understandably projects of this size required thousands of labourers. They were expected to work in shifts, and the job still took about twenty years to complete. Much of the work was done by conscripts or prisoners of war. Perhaps this was the only way the pharaohs thought they could get such vast projects completed.

Inside this gigantic piece of masonry a small but beautiful sepulchral chamber was made. Here the pharaoh would be buried when he died. Next to him would be placed his weapons and wealth, his gold and his throne. The whole pyramid was thus little more than an outsize grave stone. But a very impressive one.

According to the text for today God is involved in an enormous piece of construction involving millions of people. He has been building on this for several thousand years already. He likens those who believe in him to a temple, built together to glorify God.

PRAYER: PRAYER: Lord, I would like to be a part of your church. I want to belong to you.

CHURCHILL

And this is what he promised us — even eternal life.
1 JOHN 2:25

The Prime Minister Sir Winston Churchill was ill. He had contracted pneumonia. This was a most inconvenient time to be so ill. The Second World War was at its height, a war in which Churchill was one of the key figures. King George VI was very concerned and ordered the best doctor to be sent for. His name was Alexander Flemming, the man who had discovered penicillin in 1928. His care and medication saved the life of the prime minister.

Sir Winston Churchill came from a noble family. He grew up at Blenheim Palace. Once when he was a young boy he and his family were staying with friends who also lived on a large estate. One day Winston was playing in the lake when he came close to drowning. The gardener's son realized what was happening. He wasn't much older than Winston but he went in after him and saved his life. The Churchill family were very thankful to the boy and wanted to reward him in some way. Winston's father talked to the boy and his father in order to find out how best they could show their appreciation. During the course of the conversation it was mentioned that the gardener's son had a burning desire to become a doctor. However, his parents were not in a position to pay for the tuition. The Churchill family decided to see to it that the boy received all the education he needed to realize his dream. They agreed to pay all the bills. They kept their promise and watched with pleasure as their protegé put his heart and soul into his studies. He became a very able doctor. He was also intensely interested in medical research. This doctor, Alexander

Fleming, soon became famous, even outside Britain, mostly because of his pioneer work on penicillin.

After he had helped Sir Winston Churchill through his severe attack of pneumonia in World War Two the prime minister said to Fleming: 'Rarely has one man owed his life twice to the same rescuer.'

PRAYER: Thank you, Lord, for not only being able to save our lives here and now, but also because you want to give us eternal life.

CROSS FIRE

I will praise you, O Lord my God, with all my heart . . . . For great is your love towards me; you have delivered my soul from the depths of the grave.
PSALM 86:12, 13

There had been unrest in the Ethiopian capital, Addis Ababa, for some time. A revolution was in progress. Battles in the resulting civil war made it unsafe to be out on the streets, and it was hard to find enough food and other provisions. A young Swedish nurse had just arrived in Addis. She was to spend a few days in the capital to stock up on supplies before being driven by lorry to a small mission outpost where she was to run a clinic. Out in the sticks she would have no chance to buy medicines and other medical necessities so she spent every moment combing the various shops in Addis trying to find all she needed. She was thankful to be able to get most of her shopping done without coming across any street-fighting between government soldiers and opposition groups. The air was tense all the time, though, and the people nervous and anxious.

At last everything was bought and all was ready for her to leave the capital. The lorry was loaded that would drive her south next morning at 7. But everything was not ready. The lorry was not allowed to leave the town without a whole series of official papers and stamps because of the revolution. It took the whole morning to get all the necessary permits and it was after one o'clock before they could set off.

The lorry driver hadn't driven more than a short distance inside Addis when he was forced to stop. Battles were raging in all the streets, and the whole place was in turmoil. People were shooting and fighting all round the lorry. The police had set up road blocks to prevent the insurrection from spreading into the suburbs. The lorry driver and the young nurse just had to sit tight in the middle of the cross fire, waiting and hoping that God would protect them and their precious load. The nurse felt fear beginning to mount. 29

How was she going to manage? Was she to die without even reaching the clinic she had been called to run? She was powerless to do anything to improve her situation, so she turned to God and asked for protection and relief from fear. And God heard her. To her astonishment she became completely calm despite the desperate battle raging all around her. She picked up her little battery-driven tape recorder and played some of her favourite hymns. God was so close that she felt safe and secure during all those hours of waiting. Not till almost nightfall could the lorry set off on its long journey, people and baggage safe.

PRAYER: Be with those who today are living in fear and under the threat of war.

WHAT A PILOT!
And we urge you . . . encourage the timid, help the weak
. . . . Be joyful always.
1 THESSALONIANS 5:14, 16

Douglas Bader loved flying. He was a pilot in the Royal Air Force. He loved flying fast, doing precision dives and quick manoeuvres. He was a man who loved life and was always cheerful. But he was happiest when flying high up through the clouds, or executing some new, seemingly impossible way of flying.

One day when he was practising new stunts at very low altitude he couldn't regain sufficient height fast enough and he crashed to the ground. For a long time after the crash all he was conscious of was the terrible pain in his legs. The doctors did the only thing possible if his life was to be saved — they amputated both of his smashed legs. His friends wondered what Douglas would be like now that his life had been changed so radically. Would he continue to be just as cheerful and optimistic as before? It soon became evident that he was the same happy person even without his legs.

As soon as the stumps of his legs were healed he wanted to learn to walk with artificial legs. During the 1930s these were made of metal and not as comfortable and flexible as they are nowadays. Nevertheless, it didn't take Douglas long to learn to walk on legs of metal. Then he wanted to go back to his old job. Flying. He wanted to continue to be a pilot. But the men in charge said no. They were sure that pilots without legs could not manoeuvre planes. So he had to abide by their decision and work on the ground. When the Second World War started Douglas Bader appealed to his boss to be allowed to *prove* that he could manage a plane despite his handicap. He passed the test with flying colours and became one of the most skilled pilots defending Britain. He was eventually put in charge of five air squadrons.

Later in life he was knighted. The Queen knighted him not because of his skill and bravery during the war, nor because he could fly so well. He was knighted because he put so much time and effort into spreading joy and the will to keep on fighting to others who had handicaps. His own eagerness, enthusiasm and courage were infectious and rubbed off onto others.

PRAYER: Lord, you who want Christians to be happy, encouraging others, help me to be like that today.

RAMU

And we, who with unveiled faces all reflect the Lord's glory, are being transformed into his likeness with ever-increasing glory, which comes from the Lord.
2 CORINTHIANS 3:18

A small notice in a newspaper in March 1985 states simply that Ramu had died. Ramu was a little Indian boy, and a boy like many others in India. There are quite a few orphanages in that vast country, but Ramu didn't know about them. What actually happened to him when he was very small is a mystery. Somehow, at a very early age, he found himself in the wilderness, alone and abandoned.

Yet he was taken care of, protected and provided with food. Not by humans. By wolves. Why they took on the boy no one knows, but they did. They let him grow up as one of their own young. And he soon learned to behave just like a wolf cub, walking on all fours and doing what they did.

One day Ramu was found by people who wanted to help him. He couldn't understand these beings who wore clothes and were clean and combed. He couldn't speak a word. He had never heard anyone speak. He could only howl like a wolf. Ramu was taken to one of Mother Teresa's homes for children. There they tried to teach him to walk upright, to eat from a plate, to say useful words, to wash himself. It was no easy job. Ramu had lived like an animal for so long that he found it very difficult to leave behind him the freedom he had enjoyed in the wilds. No matter how kind people were to him he couldn't resist going out on occasional forages. However hard they tried to teach him to speak he never learnt to do so, even though he must have been about 10 years old and able to learn. Then he became ill and died while still only a child; still like those he had been with most — his wolf family.

Paul says in today's text that we will become like the Lord if we take time to be with him. We can even reflect some of his glory.

PRAYER: I want to be more like you, Lord. Make me more interested in being with you in prayer and daily Bible study.

JIGSAW PUZZLE

O Lord, you have searched me and you know me. You know when I sit and when I rise; you perceive my thoughts from afar. . . . you are familiar with all my ways.
PSALM 139:1-3

Have you ever put together a really big jigsaw puzzle? The largest one I completed consisted of 3,000 small pieces. It took an awful long time. It lay out on the table for over a week, and everyone in the family would look at it and try to fit in pieces. Because there were such large areas where the colours were practically the same it was quite confusing. All the bits with bright coloured autumn leaves seemed to fit in almost anywhere, and yet it was usually the last piece we tested which was the correct one! Without a picture to go by this puzzle would have been impossible. When I was about 8 someone gave me a home-made wooden jigsaw puzzle with a Bible picture on it. There were only about 200 pieces but there was no picture with it. It was a case of try and try again to make the pieces fit.

Life is often like putting together a puzzle without having a finished picture to go by. We are all unique, we develop differently, have different family backgrounds, different talents and plans for the future. There can be no pattern or model for us to copy which would fit everybody. But when you believe in God and trust his guidance you don't need to feel worried when you are putting together the pieces of the puzzle which form your life. God knows what the final picture will be like, even if we sometimes find it hard to know where to place certain pieces. We wonder why we had to move house. Why a close relative has died. Why we were not clever or good enough to be chosen for a particular job. Life is full of questions we can't answer. It takes time before we can see things in the right perspective and understand how the pieces in the puzzle fit together. But God knows where all the pieces should go. If we let him lead us in all we undertake he will help us to build up a life which will give us joy and satisfaction. After all, he only wants the best for us.

Sometimes we go through periods when it seems we have only dark pieces to place, but there will be brighter areas too. Trust the Master Designer.

PRAYER: Thank you for wanting to make my life into something beautiful. Help me to trust your design more.

KNOCKED TO THE FLOOR

Be still before the Lord and wait patiently for him.
PSALM 37:7

Young Margot admired her aunt very much. She was a missionary and had worked for many years as a nurse among the sick, under-nourished people of Africa. Every time Margot's aunt came home on furlough the young girl was as keen as ever to hear about life in Africa. When her aunt died, after having been a missionary for seventeen years, Margot decided that she would follow in her footsteps. As soon as she finished school she left her homeland, Sweden, and went to America to study at a missionary college. She wanted to be a nurse.

When she arrived in America she had no money for fees and knew very little English. She got a job as a home help in a wealthy family while she tried to learn English so that she could start nursing school. But the work filled nearly all her day. She hardly had time to improve her English, and the pay gave her little chance of saving for college. What could she do?

One evening when she was home alone she heard someone sneaking around the house. It was two burglars who knew the family was away. They were alarmed at finding her there. But she had managed to phone and alert a neighbour before they hit her on the head. She was hit so hard that she was on the verge of unconsciousness. A neighbour and the police came, and Margot was taken to hospital. The doctor advised her to find another job. Moving to another part of America she settled with people who knew her family in Sweden.

The new family were so pleased to have her. She was just what they needed. As soon as she had recovered from the incident with the burglars they made an agreement with her: she would help with the children and they would pay her to go to English classes. Then she could start her nurses' training. And that's how it worked out. In the end she was sure that without that unpleasant experience she would never have had the chance to study nursing and get where she wanted to be — Africa.

PRAYER: Lord, help me to be still before you, patiently waiting for your leading, not becoming discouraged when things seem to go wrong.

BABY-SITTING

The eyes of the Lord are on the righteous and his ears are attentive to their cry; . . . The righteous cry out, and the Lord hears them; he delivers them from all their troubles.
PSALM 34:15, 17

When I was in my early teens I thought looking after other people's children was fun. Not just sitting in the house in the evenings when parents were away, but during the day when I could play with the children. I was particularly fond of three small children who belonged to a missionary family. The parents were in England on leave. The father studying the Bible, and the mother receiving specialized care from the London Hospital for Tropical Medicine. During their years in the Belgian Congo, as it was called then, she had contracted several serious tropical illnesses which made her weak and tired. Because of this she was always pleased to see me when I went round to give her a hand with the children. When she needed to rest I would pile all three kiddies into a big old pram and take them over to a nearby farm to watch the cows, something they never seemed to tire of.

One day when I came home from school I said to my mother, 'I think I'll go round to the Palms' and play with the children.' My mother said that it wouldn't do me any harm to stay home for once and do some homework. She added, 'You mustn't go there too often. You know how tired Mrs. Palm is.' I went to my room with my homework but I couldn't concentrate. I kept thinking about those children and feeling more and more strongly that I should go to them. Eventually Mum agreed and I went to where the Palms lived, which was about a kilometre from my home. When Mrs. Palm saw me she said with joy and relief, 'I have been praying to God that you would come today. I feel so unwell I simply must have some help with the children.'

At that time neither she nor I had a telephone so she had no way of contacting me. The Lord saw her predicament and cared enough about it to pass on the message. It was wonderful to feel that I was the answer to someone else's prayer, to be part of God's way of helping them.

It has been said that we are God's hands and feet on this earth. What a privilege it is to be asked to go on his errands. By being keenly sensitive to what God is trying to say you may be able to do something for someone, something that Jesus would have done for that person if he had been on earth.

PRAYER: Lead me today to someone who needs me, and help me to be more willing to live for others.

LINDA

Do not slander one another.
JAMES 4:11

One day a considerable amount of money disappeared from the staff room of a Christian boarding school. The thief had done a clever job, leaving no traces behind. There were no clues to help find the culprit, that is, not until John remembered that he had seen Linda in the staff room, all on her own, on what he thought was the same day the money had disappeared. Linda must have something to do with the theft, he thought. He said so to one of his friends, who before long had mentioned it to someone else. Soon all the pupils knew about it, and what's more they had decided that Linda must be the guilty one. They informed the principal.

Linda was called for questioning. Time and again she was asked what she had done in the staff room on that particular day. She could give no good reason for having gone into the staff room when it was empty, and this made things all the more suspicious.

As the days passed and people talked, the pupils became more and more convinced that Linda was a thief. They began to avoid her and made it very plain that they disliked her, though no one said so outright. It made no difference that Linda kept telling everyone she was innocent. The pupils had put together their circumstancial evidence and that was that.

Some weeks later the preceptor for the boys' dormitory came across the thief — one of the older boys in the school. The pupils were surprised, and more than a little ashamed of how they had treated Linda. They realized they had judged and condemned her without any real evidence. Unfortunately the damage was already done and it was not easy to repair. The major problem was that the students had for so long seen Linda as a deceitful person, a thief, that it was hard to change their way of looking at her. In their minds they knew she was innocent, but it was so hard to start all over again and treat her as they had before the money disappeared. Linda remained isolated and lonely for the rest of the school year.

As Christians we should be careful not to judge someone when it only *seems* as if something adds up. By having misgivings about someone and passing them on we can spoil an innocent person's reputation and happiness completely. We should be as careful of other people's reputations as we are of our own, if not more so.

PRAYER: Help me not to judge others or speak unkindly of them. Help me to ask for forgiveness if I have already hurt someone, and help me to put it right.

PRAYER AND FASTING

Alarmed, Jehoshaphat resolved to enquire of the Lord, and he proclaimed a fast for all Judah. The people of Judah came together to seek help from the Lord.
2 CHRONICLES 20:3, 4

Nurse Margot worked at a primitive bush clinic. There wasn't much in the way of modern equipment but there was plenty of skill, love and patience. Margot was alone at the clinic, with no one to consult when complicated cases arrived needing urgent help. There was only God to whom she could go for help.

One day two parents came to the clinic with a small girl of 18 months. The child was very ill. She was too weak to hold her head up. The parents explained to Margot that she had had a sore throat and swollen tonsils and that they had taken her to the medicine man. He had put a lot of effort into rubbing foul-smelling medicaments hard into the child's neck. The result of this treatment was that the tonsils were now inflamed and filled with pus.

Margot took the little girl and tried to think of a way to help the pus run off so as to relieve the pressure in the throat. She had no suitable tube. The baby was so small. Eventually, with improvised equipment, she managed to release some of the pus, but the child was so weak that she contracted pneumonia. Now it was even more vital to get fluids into the child so that the fever wouldn't cause her to dehydrate. With the aid of a tiny tube Margot was able to feed liquids past the inflamed tonsils, but it caused the child great pain.

Three weeks passed and the fever refused to abate. The baby's throat was still inflamed, but the swelling was subsiding and it was easier to get the feeding tube down. By now the child had totally lost the ability to swallow and needed the tube the whole time. One Thursday a group of pastors came to the mission compound to hold some meetings. Margot told them about the little girl who just didn't seem to be getting better and the group promised to fast and pray for the child. They kept their promise, praying all night. The next morning when Margot was making a thin gruel to feed the baby, one of the pastors saw her and came across. He said he was sure God had heard their prayers and that the child was healed. Together they went to look at the little girl. It was true! The fever had gone, and what was even more exciting, the girl could swallow again. Margot put away the tube. Now she could feed her with a spoon. It wasn't too long before the little girl was strong enough to learn to walk.

PRAYER: Thank you, Lord, that it was not just in Bible times that people could turn to you for help. We can still do so today.

THE HAND IN THE DARK

**Praise the Lord, O my soul, and forget not all his benefits
. . . he redeems my life from the pit and crowns me with
love and compassion.**
PSALM 103:2, 4

For the eighth time Pastor Svensson got out of his car by the side
of the road in order to clear his windscreen. His wipers had gone
on strike and large wet snowflakes insisted on staying put on his
windscreen, and they kept coming in ever-increasing amounts. It
was hardly possible to drive as he could see practically nothing
in the snow and darkness. He wondered how many more times
he would have to stop and clean his windscreen before he arrived
home. It was already getting very late and he was tired after the
long evangelistic meeting that evening.

What with the darkness and the heavy snow and the unfamiliar
road through the Swedish woods, the pastor soon became unsure
as to where he was. He was sure he was on the right road, but
he did wonder where the sharp curve was which he had noticed
when he drove to the meeting that afternoon. Had he really driven
so slowly and stopped so often that he hadn't reached that curve
yet? It was possible though still rather strange. But there was nothing for it but to continue. He must get to his lodgings. It was
too cold to sleep in the car.

He sat there tense and alone, trying to see where the road went.
If he drove off it he would end up in the deep snow-covered
verge. That mustn't happen. Suddenly he saw a hand reach out
towards his steering wheel. The hand placed itself on his hand,
very firmly. Before the pastor had time to wonder what this could
mean, a voice said: 'Stop!' Pastor Svensson stood on his brakes
and the car stopped. The hand was gone, and however much he
looked in the car there was no sign of anyone, and no footprints
outside when he jumped out to check. Once out of the car he
forgot all about the hand in the dark. His whole attention was
caught by something else. He saw that his headlights were not
lighting up the road or the verge but were pointing out into
nowhere. Bewildered, he went to see why this was. To his horror
he saw that his car stood on the very edge of a steep drop. There
was no fence across the road which could have prevented him
from driving over the edge and down to his death. In the heavy
snow he had driven the wrong way and had ended up on a small
road through the forest, a road down to a gravel pit. He hadn't
known where he was, but God knew.

*PRAYER: Thank you for seeing us wherever we are, and for using your
power to save us from danger. Help us to trust in you.*

TURUMBO

" 'We . . . will cry out . . . in our distress, and you will hear us and save us.' "

2 CHRONICLES 20:9

Turumbo had contracted the dreaded typhus fever. Quite a lot of people in Africa get this serious and often fatal sickness due to the fact that their drinking water isn't clean. Turumbo was only 8 years old and her parents carried her to the only place where there was any form of medical help available, the simple little clinic that nurse Margot ran all alone. When they reached the clinic the girl was barely conscious. It was evening and the two beds in the clinic were already occupied by other very sick patients. What was Margot to do? She badly wanted to try to save the girl's life. A simple bed was arranged in a nearby hut. The next day Turumbo was much worse, and lay in a coma.

Margot asked God what she should do, and the idea came to her to use the operating table as an extra bed and to fix up a drip-feed bottle from a hook. Turumbo's parents stood one on each side of the table so that she wouldn't fall off in her delirious state. There was not much more Margot could do at this point. She had to attend to the seventy or more out-patients who were waiting for treatment. When night came there was still the question of what to do with the little girl. She couldn't stay where she was. Margot prayed again and this time she had the idea of using the empty waiting room as an extra ward. She made a soft bed for her in there and hung the drip-feed bottle from the rafters.

Days passed. Margot prayed for Turumbo and kept a close eye on her all the time. Sometimes the girl was unconscious, sometimes she seemed to be on the verge of waking. It was too early to be sure that she would make it. All Margot could do was pray and wait for the illness to run its course. But one day when Margot looked in to where Turumbo lay, she heard something which made the tears well up in her eyes: 'Mama, I'm hungry.' The crisis was over. Turumbo had made it despite the primitive conditions and the lack of hospital treatment. As Margot says: 'God can heal the sick even in small clinics.'

PRAYER: Lord, be with those today who are suffering and are sick. May they feel that you are near them to support and help them.

THE GHOST SHIP

**He who doubts is like a wave of the sea, blown and
tossed by the wind.**
JAMES 1:6

There was joy on the ship which sailed far out on the Atlantic.
Another ship had been sighted on the horizon. It would be good
to see some other human beings and perhaps hear fresh news.
The year was 1872 and in those days news came from passing
boats coming from foreign ports. As they drew nearer the ship
they began to signal greetings. No answering signals came. How
strange! Was there no one on the bridge to keep a look out?

As the ship drew closer to this strange boat the captain could
see through his telescope that she was called the *Marie Céleste*.
There was no one visible on deck. Very remarkable indeed. This
needed looking into. They went as close to the big vessel as possible and began to call loudly to the crew in case they were below
deck. Still no one answered. As far as they could see there was
nothing wrong with the vessel. The sails and rigging were as they
should be.

They decided to board the *Marie Céleste* to see what was wrong.
Not many of the crew were willing to climb aboard this ghost-like
ship, but those who dared found much which couldn't be explained. They searched the whole vessel but found none of the
twenty-six men who had signed on the ship according to the papers
on the captain's desk. They looked closely at the ship herself to
see if there was any sign of a battle having taken place, but everything seemed in order. They read the ship's log to see if they could
find any clue to what had happened. The last entry had been made
ten days previously, but even in that entry nothing unusual was
written. The *Marie Céleste* had become a ghost ship which floated
along without any goal. It was a depressing sight — a fine ship,
completely undamaged, just being driven by the whims of the wind,
far out at sea.

*PRAYER: Help me not to drift through life, Lord. Grant me a faith that
can help me do something worth while.*

A VERY OLD LADY

" 'Love your neighbour as yourself.' "
MATTHEW 22:39

Have you at any time found it hard to like a particular person?
If so, perhaps you have got round the problem by avoiding the
person in question, but sometimes this is not possible. Some years
ago I worked in a small church where everybody knew everybody

else very well. The atmsophere was that of one large happy family most of the time. But there was one problem, or to put it another way, there was one problematic woman. She was very old and difficult to get on with. Try as I might I found it hard to like her. She always wanted to get into heated debates and was critical of everything that others did. It was impossible to avoid her — she saw to that personally. I tried to be kind to her but it was a real effort.

I realized I would have to do something about this situation, so I began to pray about it. I simply asked the Lord to help me like this belligerent old woman. Some days later, after the church service, I had to wait an hour for my bus home. The old lady decided to stay behind and keep me company while I waited. I wondered how it would end, and I kept praying silently, until I noticed that I no longer needed to do so. She began to tell me about herself, and during that hour managed to cover a lot of ground. She spoke about her problems and her view of things. By the time the bus came I felt quite differently about her. I had been given a chance to see her from another angle. God answered my prayer by giving me time to get to know someone he cared about and wanted me to care about too.

This made me feel so happy. During the following years I still had problems with her now and again, finding it hard to like her at times. But God seemed to be very anxious that I did like her, because every time I prayed to God for help with this woman he gave me new opportunities to know her better.

Why don't you try this too? Pray to get on better with someone you find hard to have around. It does work.

PRAYER: Help me to like the people I meet every day, and if I can't, help me to see them through your loving eyes.

IN THE UNDERGROUND

For he will command his angels concerning you
to guard you in all your ways.
PSALM 91:11

It was late in the evening. Rosemary, an attractive 20-year-old, was going to take the underground home from a central point in Stockholm. She had often done so without any problem. This particular evening when she came down to the platform the place was empty except for a gang of restless teenage boys. Rosemary was obliged to walk past them in order to get where she had to wait for her train. It seemed at first as though the youths hadn't really noticed her as she stood there at the far end of the platform trying to be as inconspicuous as possible.

After a while she noticed that the gang was looking her way, talking more loudly and laughing in a spine-chilling fashion. The group moved closer to her and she began to be afraid. There was still no one else on the platform. Rosemary turned her back on the youths and pretended to be reading the adverts, but she was praying for God's protection. The gang was quite close to her now. As she kept praying she became aware that the boys had become very subdued and she turned her head to see what was going on. To her great relief she saw a middle-aged man with a briefcase standing between her and the boys. He had his back to her and was keeping the youths under observation. There were two trains due before the one that Rosemary was to catch. She now began to pray that the man would stay there till her train came. His presence had such a curbing effect on the gang.

The first train came and went, and the man remained. Ten minutes later the next train came. The man stood in the same place. The third train. What a relief that this man was to catch the same train, thought Rosemary, and told the Lord so, thankfully.

At last the train came. She jumped on quickly and watched to see the man board the train. But no one did. She looked along the platform. The gang of boys was leaving. She looked again at the place where the man had stood. He wasn't there, nor anywhere along the whole platform.

PRAYER: Thank you, Lord, for the protection your angels give us. Usually we don't see them, but we know you have promised to be with us always.

A SACRIFICE

But now he (Christ) has appeared ... to do away with sin by the sacrifice of himself.
HEBREWS 9:26

In history books we read about terrible epidemics which in earlier times raged in different countries. They were usually called 'the plague' and thousands of people met a terrible death. In those days there was not much the doctors could do. This was mainly because they knew too little about the illness and there was no way of researching to find a cure.

When the plague raged in the city of Marseilles in France, all the doctors in the town gathered to discuss what could be done. They had to stop the deaths. After much debating they came to the conclusion that the only way to understand the disease was to examine the body of someone who had died of the plague. All the doctors in the room knew that whoever performed this examination would soon die from the highly contagious illness. The room remained silent for a long time. Finally a young doctor stood up. He was a very able doctor and had done well in his career so far. Without hesitation he explained that he was willing to examine someone who had died of the plague. He was willing to make the sacrifice for the sake of his fellow countrymen so that the devastating effects of the plague might be stopped and peoples' lives saved.

He left the hall and wrote his will. That same night he examined a victim of the plague. He wrote down all he found which might be of help, then put the paper into a jar of vinegar so that the person who read it wouldn't become contaminated. The doctor, whose name was Guyon, caught the plague and died after twelve hours of agony.

We think that people who are willing to sacrifice their lives for others are very praiseworthy, and of course they are. We always hope that their sacrifice was not in vain but of benefit to other people. When Jesus gave his life on the cross it was to save people from something which had even worse consequences than the plague — sin, which can cause people to be lost forever.

PRAYER: Thank you, Jesus for giving your life for me. I accept your gift of salvation. You didn't die in vain.

APRIL FOOL'S DAY

**Help us, O God our Saviour ... and atone for our sins
for your name's sake.**
PSALM 79:9

Let's do something really different for April Fool's Day this year, decided a group of pupils at a small village school. It was the kind of school where several classes are held in the same room, and everybody knows everyone else very well, including the teachers.

The pupils of the higher forms set about planning. Gradually the idea developed. Something should be done to get at the head teacher who was rather strict, and therefore not always the most popular teacher. One bright spark suggested she be made so sleepy that she would fall asleep during class. This would be very funny — at least it was different! They decided to add something to the hot drink that the students made for the teachers every morning at break time. But what should they put in the drink?

One of the pupils remembered that his grandmother used strong sleeping tablets at night because she had a lot of pain. He said he would try to get hold of one of these tablets by the first of April. The day came, the tablet was on hand, but the head teacher was absent. It was such an anticlimax after so much planning that they decided to use it on the French teacher instead. The drink was prepared and to the pupils' delight the teacher drank half of it. She was to teach the class after break, so there would be ample time to study her reactions and have some fun.

Before the lesson was due to finish she was so drowsy and felt so queer that she went to her room to lie down. It so happened that she lived close by the school. When she didn't reappear after lunch one of the other teachers went to see her. She was sleeping so soundly that she was on the verge of being deeply unconscious. A doctor had to be called to give the French teacher an injection which would counteract the substance in the sleeping tablet to which she was obviously over-sensitive. She was poorly for several days. The joke had almost ended in tragedy.

When everyone had been questioned and the truth had come out, the head teacher mentioned that if the tablet had been given to her, as was originally planned, she would have died as she was allergic to those tablets. What had started as a joke had a very bitter ending.

PRAYER: Thank you for forgiving us our wrong-doings. Help us to be more careful how we treat others, even when we are joking.

COLOURED COFFINS

We do not want you to be ignorant about those who fall asleep, or to grieve like the rest of men, who have no hope.
1 THESSALONIANS 4:13

Different peoples and cultures have varying customs about funerals and about what happens to the dead. When, for example, the Egyptian Pharaohs died they were buried with all their worldly wealth so that they would enjoy a good status in the kingdom of the dead. In other cultures, about 2,000 years or more ago, when a person died and was buried his servants and his dogs were buried with him so that he would have all the help he needed in the other world to which he had gone.

In the little town in Ghana where I lived for a while you could see, set out neatly on the pavement, all kinds of beautiful coffins. It was interesting to look at them. They were true works of art and painted in the brightest colours imaginable. The sides could be yellow, the top red. The coffins were always displayed open, so that passers-by could see how comfortable they were. There were soft cushions and padding in all shades and designs. On both long sides of the coffin there were small windows, so that the dead person could see where he was going. Each little window had pretty curtains. In this town people went round to look for the coffin they thought was most beautiful and most comfortable. When they had found the right one they bought it for themselves. 43

That way they were sure that when they died they would be comfortable!

When someone in this Ghanaian town died a big feast was arranged, with singing and dancing, which lasted a whole night. When the person who had died was buried great care was taken that his feet pointed towards his home village. The idea was that when the dead woke up they would be able to find their way back home.

Many people have their own concepts of what happens when we die. But these are only speculations, because no one knows exactly. Only God knows, and he has explained it in the Bible. There death is likened to a sleep from which we awake when Jesus comes back on the resurrection day.

PRAYER: Lord, you alone know all about life and death. Help me to trust you completely so that I will not fear the unknown, because you are there too.

MALARIA

Even though I walk through the valley of the shadow of death, I will fear no evil, for you are with me; your rod and staff, they comfort me.
PSALM 23:4

When you are the only nurse at a little clinic miles out in the middle of nowhere in the African bush there are many things you have to be able to manage all alone. There is no one, other than God, to whom you can go for advice. You often have to make do with improvisation in a country where medical equipment simply cannot be bought. It gives you a great thrill every time such means, plus prayer, prove to be successful in the saving of lives. But what happens when you get sick yourself and there is no other medical person within at least 100km?

Nurse Margot had a very high temperature. She quite often fell sick, becoming infected by the people she worked among, but mostly recovered quite quickly. This time it was something more serious — malaria. Margot's friends, who knew nothing about medicine, decided to take her down to the little airstrip from which planes sporadically left for the capital. There was no proper road from the clinic down to the airstrip so they were forced to transport the sick nurse half lying on the back of a donkey. By this time Margot's temperature had been over 39°C for quite some time and she was very weak. After a long and painful donkey ride the little group arrived at the airstrip.

The little runway looked deserted. Could they have come on 44 the wrong day? Didn't the DC-3 always come on a Tuesday? They went and asked in the little hut which acted as the ticket office. The answer was that there would be no flight for three weeks! What a message when you are seriously ill! All they could do was lead the donkey back up to the clinic and hope that the sick nurse would survive until the next plane was due.

I asked Margot later whether she was afraid when she lay there on the point of death, without help or the right medicines to take for the unusual form of malaria she had contracted. 'No', she replied. 'I could leave everything in God's hands, even death. I felt all the time that God was very close to me. It was a strange and wonderful experience.'

The three weeks passed and it was time for the next donkey trip down to the airstrip. By this time Margot was even weaker, but somehow she put up with the hardship. The plane came and she was flown to the capital where she received immediate help. It wasn't long before she was back at her post again, weak, but very keen to work.

PRAYER: Thank you for being close to those who are having a hard time, especially when they have no other help. Help us to trust that you will be at hand even when death's shadows are near.

IN THE LAST MINUTE

The Lord told him, "Go to the house of Judas on Straight Street and ask for a man from Tarsus named Saul, for he is praying."
ACTS 9:11

The pastor was tired and hungry after a long and difficult day. He was just about to hang up his overcoat when he seemed to hear a voice within him saying, 'Go to the third house on the left of the street.' The pastor was somewhat surprised because he didn't know anyone who lived in the street. He thought to himself that he could go there later and have a look, once he had eaten and rested for a while. Before he had even finished this thought the voice impressed him again, saying, 'Go now, go at once.' He knew the voice well, having heard and obeyed it many times before. So he put his coat back on and set off to look for the house.

How strange, he thought, once he found it. It looked completely empty. He went up to the door and knocked. Nobody answered and he turned round to go back down to the gate. He hadn't walked very far before the voice urged him to go and knock once more. He did so, but no one came and opened the door. The house seemed to be completely uninhabited. He turned to go again, wondering what the Lord was asking him to do there. A third time he was impressed to knock on the door. This time it was opened by a very frightened and sick young woman. The pastor didn't really know what to say, so he just explained simply that God had asked him to come to this house and knock on the door.

The young woman stared at the pastor for a long while. Her face showed both astonishment and a kind of relief. 'So there is a God', she said very quietly after a long silence. She invited the pastor in. The house was practically empty of furniture. Three small children sat on the bare floor in the living room. Once the woman had talked a little more with the pastor and become convinced that God had really sent him to her, she took out four open bottles of lemonade. She told the pastor that she had put a lethal dose of poison in these bottles. She and the children were just about to drink this when the pastor had knocked on the door the first time. The woman explained tearfully that everything had gone wrong for her and that she felt she couldn't live any longer and that there didn't seem to be anyone willing to help her.

Now she experienced that there was a God who cared about her and her children, and a church which was willing to support her and help her to start a new and happier life. All this came about just because *one* person was sensitive to the Lord's voice.

PRAYER: Lord, help me to hear what you want to say to me. Make me willing to help others.

SUNSET

Do not let the sun go down while you are still angry.
EPHESIANS 4:26

Anne went out and slammed the door hard behind her. Not to make it lock but to show her mother that she was angry, very angry. She planned to stay away from home for a while so that mother would start to worry. She would get her own back on her mother for interfering in her business. Anne was 13 now and quite sure she could manage everything on her own. What did mother have to do with things? Anne had become so angry that she had shouted horrible things at her mother. Mother had looked sad but hadn't reacted. Her calm had only made Anne the more angry. Now she was going out and wasn't going to come back for ages.

She cycled off in the warm afternoon sun. Spring had come and everything smelt lovely and the birds were singing. Anne noticed all this but, being determined, only started to cycle faster. She had decided where she was going — to a small ridge down by the river. No one would disturb her there and she would be able to think in peace. When she reached the ridge she threw down her bike and lay in the fresh green grass. How could she teach her mother that she, Anne, didn't need to be told things anymore? How could she punish her mother so that she would leave her in peace in future? Anne lay there and thought about all the rows they had had lately. How difficult mother was being! Just to think that she would have to live with her for several more years before she could leave home was awful.

Time passed and Anne was still out on the ridge. They will have had tea by now, she thought. But she was too worked up to feel hungry. She sat and looked towards the west. The sun was going down, becoming more and more red and beautiful the lower it sank. The few clouds on the skyline turned pink. It was all so lovely that for a moment Anne forgot why she was there. Then she suddenly remembered the text the pastor had preached on not so long ago. A strange text about sunsets and anger. The pastor had said that it meant you should make up the same day, and not let an argument remain unresolved till the next day. Put things right before the sun goes down. It's easiest and best that way, he had said.

Anne didn't remain sitting there until the sun had gone down below the horizon. She reached home before that, and hugged her mother. It felt good to have things put right before it was time to go to bed.

PRAYER: *Lord, help me not to be too proud to ask for forgiveness when I have been angry or unpleasant.*

PUTTING THINGS RIGHT

The Lord said ... " 'When a man or woman wrongs another in any way ... that person is guilty and must confess the sin he has committed. He must make full restitution for his wrong.' "
NUMBERS 5:5-7

Alex sat in his cell and thought about what the prison priest had said. If you believed in God, he had said, then God would help you to withstand the temptation to steal. Alex had been in prison for over a year now after being arrested for armed robbery. I should like to live an ordinary, honest life, he thought. He prayed to God and thought that now he was a Christian everything would be fine and he would no longer be tempted. Things would automatically go right for him. But a few days after being set free he had carried out an even worse crime and been arrested again.

Back behind bars he was angry with himself and with God. He was really disappointed with God. Why hadn't God prevented this? Alex decided never again even to think of doing what was right, let alone care whether there was a God or not. After some time 47 he began to plan his escape from prison. He succeeded in escaping, left England, and went across to France and joined the Foreign Legion. However, though Alex may have left God, God had not left him. As time passed it began to dawn on Alex that he had never really come to know the Lord personally, never mind allow God to live in his heart. God spoke time and again to him through his conscience. Alex began to realize why things had gone so wrong before. He gave his heart and life completely to God and asked him for forgiveness for all the wrongs he had committed. God forgave him and gave him a wonderful sense of peace.

What should Alex do now? He felt that as a Christian he should put right his earlier wrongs. He left the Foreign Legion, made his way to the British Embassy in Paris, and told them who he was and what he had been imprisoned for. This wasn't an easy thing for Alex to do, but he wanted to have a clear conscience. He was shipped back to England and put in prison to sit out the rest of his long sentence. You would be tempted to think that Alex would be disappointed in God again, given that God didn't arrange for him to be freed. Not at all. Alex's faith grew stronger instead. I know a pastor who visits him in prison, not so much to encourage Alex as to be inspired and encouraged by this dedicated prisoner whose convictions are so strong that they are contagious.

PRAYER: Please, Lord, give me the courage to put right what I have done wrong, even if I have to take the consequences for my wrong-doing.

TETANUS

You are the God who performs miracles.
PSALM 77:14

Two men made their way along the jungle path. They walked carefully because they were carrying a very sick 11-year-old boy on a home-made stretcher. The boy was almost unconscious. It was important to get to the clinic soon. The boy's father had died some time earlier so it was an uncle who was going along with him. The man knew nothing about medicine, but he had heard that the little clinic was good.

When they reached the clinic the nurse examined the boy and told them he had tetanus. She explained to the uncle that this was a very serious illness and there was very little she could do to save the boy. If they allowed him to remain at the clinic she would look after him as well as was possible, but she could give no promises. However, the uncle had decided that all the boy needed was an injection. Then he had planned to carry him back home. Nurse Margot explained that this would mean certain death. The uncle refused to listen. After they had left, Margot just couldn't forget the sick boy. She felt she should pray for him even if he was no longer her patient.

Two days later the same two men came back with the same stretcher. The boy was almost dead, and now the uncle wanted Margot to look after him. She knew it was just about hopeless, but she was the type of person who never gave up hope regarding sick patients. She placed the boy in a dark room and fed him round the clock on fluids poured down a tube into his stomach. She spent time cooking nourishing soups for him in an effort to give his body a little strength to fight this dangerous illness. Sometimes the boy had severe attacks of cramp and she had to give him injections. After some weeks he became strong enough to eat a little with a spoon and after a month it seemed as though he would make it. But then suddenly his heart stopped. Margot prayed while she gave the thin little body heart massage. To her great joy the heart started up again. He suffered heart failure several more times, but each time Margot was on hand and could get his heart going again. After three months the boy was fully recovered. Now he had been among Christians for many weeks and had started to think about his own future. He decided to start at a mission school and learn about God and other things. By the end of the first school year he felt he knew God so well that he wanted to be baptized.

PRAYER: Today, Lord, I want to pray for all those who are working as missionaries, often all alone. Please help and support them.

THE RECORDING SESSION

The Lord is near to all who call on him. . . . He fulfils the desires of those who fear him; he hears their cry and saves them.
PSALM 145:18, 19

Some years ago I had a part in making a record with three Christian young people from Finland. They were to sing religious songs and I was to accompany them on the piano. We had succeeded in getting hold of a good recording studio in Helsinki and had been allotted time one evening. It cost quite a bit to hire the studio so we were trying to get things recorded as fast as possible.

This turned out to be easier said than done! One thing after the other went wrong. First of all the piano couldn't be used as it was — it made a loud click every time the pedal was raised. In a great hurry a piano tuner was found, but he couldn't mend the fault properly, only adjust things so that the click wasn't so noticeable. By this time it was getting late, after 10pm. We were all tired and there was still much to be recorded.

The next big problem arose when the soprano was to sing a

very high note in one of the songs. Every time she tried her voice broke. Between each retake we prayed together that God would help her with this high note, but there was no improvement. Why didn't God do anything? After all, weren't we recording songs about him? He ought to have cared. By now it was after 11pm and we were all on the verge of tears.

We continued by recording some of the other songs which didn't go so high. Suddenly we noticed that smoke was coming into the room from under one of the doors. Soon the recording studio was so filled with smoke that it was hard to breathe, never mind sing! We went up the steps from the basement studio to see what was going on. Out there in the street were police cars and fire-engines. It turned out to be nothing more serious than someone having thrown a smoke-bomb into the large restaurant above the studio.

Since it was evident that any further recording that night would be impossible the company gave us extra time the next morning. They also paid our hotel bill. The next morning everything went perfectly, and the job was completed in a short time. We were less nervous, having become accustomed to our surroundings by then. It turned out to be reasonable too. We didn't need to pay for the long hours we had been there the night before.

God sometimes uses very strange ways to help people, doesn't he?

PRAYER: Thank you, Lord, for always hearing us when we pray.

'ORPHANAGES, LORD?'

"I am the Lord your God .... Open wide your mouth and I will fill it."
PSALM 81:10

George Müller had studied to become a missionary or a preacher. In the year 1835 he was serving as a pastor in the town of Bristol where he became increasingly aware of the plight of orphaned children. The more he saw their sufferings the more he felt he wanted to do something for them. As he had no wage he couldn't help by giving them money. He began to pray about the matter, and as he did so a longing began to grow in his heart, a longing to give these orphaned children a home and schooling and at the same time learn about God. Great plans for someone without any money!

Müller not only prayed, he also read God's Word. One day while he was wondering if he should dare to start something for these children without financial backing, he read the text you have just read. He felt that God was telling him that if he would only give him a chance he would fill all his needs. With a thankful heart

Müller fell to his knees and prayed for a large house in which to place the children and for people who would be willing to help him in this work. He also prayed for £1,000 to pay initial expenses, wages and rents. When he had finished his prayer he waited for God's answer.

Müller was convinced that if this whole matter was actually God's idea God would supply the means without him having to go round begging for money. He did discuss his plans with friends, but he never asked them for financial support. He didn't need to ask. God impressed different people to give what they had — plates, cutlery, furniture, bed linen, and various sums of money. There was now no longer any doubt in Müller's mind that God was backing the project. Before long he was offered a large house at a low rent, and soon everything was in order, ready to receive thirty homeless children. So Müller got on his knees and prayed that the Lord would send him children who needed a home. The next day they began to come.

But thirty places was nowhere near enough if all the orphans were to be given a home. Soon Müller had to open more homes. All the time he kept the fast-growing number of children and staff fed, clothed and housed by spending time on his knees in prayer. God provided exactly the amount of material goods and cash that was needed for the day, even if it was sometimes a very close run thing. God kept the promise he had given Müller in Psalm 81:10. He filled his ever-growing needs, needs on behalf of others. Without Müller ever having to ask anyone for funds the children in his care could always be given clothes to wear and enough simple food to eat to keep them strong and well.

PRAYER: Dear Lord, be with those who do not have a home and family. Strengthen those who are trying to help the homeless.

THE POTTER

"Like clay in the hand of the potter, so are you in my hand."
JEREMIAH 18:5

In Africa I kept my filtered and pure water in a big hand-made earthenware jar. It was beautifully shaped and had been made by a man in the village near where I lived. You could go and watch him work there in the shade of a big avocado tree outside his house. He had a home-made potter's wheel which he rotated with his feet, but most of the time he chose to use only his hands when he formed his clay pots.

He dug up the clay himself. In this clay there could be all types of impurities, rubbish and small stones. These had to be removed or the clay pots would be valueless. They wouldn't just look bad, they might leak or crack. In order to prevent this the potter kneaded the lumps of clay and worked over each piece before he even thought of starting to form something with it. Sometimes he did miss some impurity or a tiny stone in the clay, and discovered this only when the pot he was making was almost completed. Then he had no choice but to take out the rubbish, knead the clay back into a lump and start all over again.

When the potter had finished forming his large and beautiful water pots they were still not ready for use, even though they might look it. They were still soft and pliable. Now they had to go through a thorough drying process in the burning hot tropical sun. The dryer the clay, the lighter the colour became and the harder and stronger the pot. Finally, when it had stood in the hot sun for many days the pot was hard and ready to be put to use. Some pots were for carrying or storing water, others for making food in. They were strong too.

The Bible says that God works with us just as gently and carefully as a potter works with his clay. God tries to form us into people who will be useful — people who are of value and a joy to others. It can feel a bit unpleasant when the Master Potter has to remove bits of 'rubbish' which would spoil our lives and give us a bad character, but at times like that remember that he is a real Craftsman. You can rely totally on him. What he forms us into will be the best we could become.

PRAYER: Lord, I want to give myself completely to you, so that you can mould me. I realize I cannot make anything good out of my life without your help.

IT COULD HAVE BEEN ME

I waited patiently for the Lord; he turned to me and heard my cry. He lifted me out of the slimy pit.
PSALM 40:1, 2

Ian couldn't believe it. He didn't want to believe it. His 18-year-old friend was dead. They had been together just the day before. This sort of thing just can't happen, Ian kept saying to himself over and over again. But it was true even if he didn't want to believe it. Ian had himself been rushed to hospital twice and been saved from the same death. But for his friend it had been too late. No one could save him.

Ian really had something to think about now. It could just as easily have been him who had died and was to be buried the next week. Perhaps it would soon be his turn if he didn't think
52 about changing certain things in his life. If he didn't try now

he would never do it. If he wasn't careful it would soon be too late for him also.

But changing his whole life-style was no easy matter. You see, Ian had been 'sniffing' for several years and felt he just couldn't stop even though he had had two serious narrow escapes. Both times he had ended up in hospital and been saved from choking to death. It was his now dead friend who had encouraged and taught Ian to sniff. It had seemed such fun in the beginning and so harmless, while at the same time being exciting because it was 'forbidden'. Now it had ended in tragedy.

Ian knew that his mother was very worried about him and that she prayed for him. Ian had never had much interest in God, but now he realized that if he was to get rid of his strong dependence on drugs he would need help, and more than mere human help. Supposing his mother was right and God could do what seems impossible? He could at least give God a chance, he thought. He began to pray seriously, and noticed that the impossible was beginning to happen. Ian found to his great joy that if he took time to pray when he felt the craving coming back, he was given the strength to withstand the temptation to 'sniff' again. Of course he did not find the way back to a healthy drug-free life easy. However, every time he turned to God for help he was helped. Now Ian is completely cured of his craving and has chosen to work for God with the talents he has given him.

PRAYER: Thank you, Lord, that nothing is impossible for you. You can pull us up out of the pit, however far down we have sunk, if only we ask for your help.

THE TRAIN TICKET

"Ask and it will be given to you; seek and you will find; . . . For everyone who asks receives; he who seeks finds."
MATTHEW 7:7, 8

There is one thing I am extremely good at, and that is losing or forgetting things. It doesn't matter if it's large or small, I can lose it! This in turn means that a lot of time needs to be spent looking for keys, brushes, or important papers.

Once I lost a return ticket for a train trip from the south of Sweden to where we were living at that time, way up in the north. The distance was about 500 miles. It was an expensive ticket! I had lost it in my parents' house where we were staying for a fortnight. We had made a concerted effort to find it, spending several days looking everywhere. We found lots of other things, but not the ticket. Time passed, and there was only one day left before the ticket was to be used on our return journey.

I asked the Lord to show me where I should look in order to find this precious ticket. I felt impressed to go down to the hall by the kitchen door. I did so and looked around carefully, but found nothing. I thought the whole episode a bit strange but said nothing to any of the family. Not long after this my husband went up and knelt by his bed, asking the Lord to show him where to find the ticket. He was also impressed to go down to the hall by the kitchen door, and went down there immediately to look. He didn't know that I had already combed through the place, and set about looking. Now when it comes to searching for things my husband and I are very different. I tend to look in all the possible places whereas he takes time to search through the impossible ones. This is how he went about it, and found the ticket — in the hall, near the kitchen door. It had somehow fallen down into an old umbrella stand which had stood in that hall for many a year. God had seen where the ticket was and given us a hint as to where to find it.

Every time I think about that particular train ticket I can't help being amazed at God. How he can find the time, and how he can show the interest in such tiny, almost insignificant, details in our lives when he has major crises to take care of in every corner of the world! He has the wonderful ability to make everyone feel he or she is special to him. Incredible!

PRAYER: Thank you, Lord, for being interested in every detail of my life, and for being willing to help me even with the small things.

THE GARDEN

The Lord will indeed give what is good, and our land will yield its harvest.
PSALM 85:12

You remember we have talked about Margot who worked as a nurse in Africa? Well, sometimes there was a shortage of the kind of food she could eat, and so she always saw to it that when she was home in Sweden visiting her parents, she would buy vegetable seeds for growing in her tropical garden. The first thing she did when she moved to a new place in Africa was to prepare a garden and sow her seeds. This would save time later on. Then she would have suitable food without having to go a long way to get it. After all, the long days at the clinic meant there was little time left over for foraging for food!

On one occasion when she moved to a new area she had a local African boy who helped her with her new garden. He lived in the village and belonged to the church there. He was so thankful for being given a job and a chance to earn a little money that he really wanted to do his best to help Mamma Margot get a good kitchen garden going. Together they turned over the land, dug in manure and then carefully sowed the precious seeds from Sweden. In the tropical heat they soon germinated and became small plants. Every day Margot went and looked at her seedlings. She really loved her garden, loved watching it come to life.

But then the monsoon rains came and washed away all the seedlings. When the ground had dried a little the garden boy sowed new seeds and these also grew very rapidly into small plants in the warm, humid air. But before their roots had become strong enough the next monsoon rains came and washed these seedlings away too. They were both so disappointed. It was a good job that Margot had brought lots of seeds, because there was nothing else to do but sow a third time. These plants didn't make it either!

The garden boy was just as sad about it as Margot. Would she never be able to grow anything to eat? Would things not be given a chance to grow strong enough to survive the coming dry season? One day the garden boy said to Margot, 'Mamma Margot, do you know what we should do? We should go out into the garden and ask God to protect the new seeds so that they will grow up properly.' Margot agreed and they went out together and knelt down in what they hoped would one day be a kitchen garden. They both prayed that God would give them the harvest they needed and then the boy sowed seeds for the fourth time. Now he was even more interested to see how they grew, and went and looked at the seedlings several times a day. To him these were no ordinary plants but plants which God was protecting. They kept on growing so fast you could almost watch them reaching up, and before long the first lettuce was ready. The plants seemed to make up for lost time. However many Margot ate there were always plenty left over. She and the garden boy began to share the produce with the neighbours and there were still plenty left. The garden boy wasn't a bit surprised — God had grown these.

PRAYER: Help me, Lord, to leave even small things in your hands.

WHAT DO YOU READ?

**Whatever is true . . . whatever is right, whatever is pure . . .
whatever is admirable . . . think about such things.**
PHILIPPIANS 4:8

John grew up in a happy home in a suburban area. His parents were Christians and they really cared about him and his younger brother Patrick. John was very interested in reading. Every time he had a spare moment he would have his nose in a book. He even read when he didn't have the time and should have been doing something else. He was so involved in what he read that he lived in a different world and didn't hear when he was being called. He spent most of his time reading about crime. These books were so exciting he could hardly put them down. It didn't make any difference how often his parents tried to talk to him about the kind of books he read. It only made him read under the covers at night.

When he was into his teens he was no longer satisfied just reading about exciting criminal acts. He started to plan his own small crimes and soon found other teenagers who were keen to go along with him. Life became exciting and dangerous — as in the books. John continued to read, not just for entertainment, but in order to learn more tricks of the trade so that he could carry out more crimes without being found out.

John and his gang began to plan more daring projects. Everything had worked well so far. His parents didn't notice anything at home other than that he was out more. Which meant that he was reading less.

One winter's evening he came rushing into the lounge. He was bleeding profusely from a gunshot wound in the arm. He was pale and his whole body shook. He was in a state of shock. His mother was afraid, especially since John wouldn't tell her what had happened and refused to allow her to call a doctor.

The next morning the police were outside the door. There was no use denying anything. The story was out. The boys had planned a burglary in a supermarket. They had been able to get hold of an old gun — the type of thing thieves always had in the books. When they were discovered by the night-watchman John was so scared that he did exactly what he had read about for all those years — he fired a shot at the watchman. Now the police came with the news that the man had died of his wound. John was arrested for murder. What had started as seemingly harmless, just the world of books, had become reality, a living nightmare. John had to spend many years in prison as a result.

PRAYER: Lord, help me to fill my thoughts with things that can help me become a better person and a more responsible citizen.

THE DRUMS

Therefore encourage one another and build each other up.
1 THESSALONIANS 5:11

Mensah had studied the Bible for several months with a neighbour who was a Christian. Prior to this Mensah had known nothing about God. He lived in West Africa and had worshipped other gods than the one in the Bible all his life. His greatest joy in life had been to participate in the frenzied night-long heathen dancing. The rhythm of the drums bewitched him. As soon as they began to sound on the damp night air he was drawn to the place of dancing whether he wanted to go or not. And he danced for hours in the warm tropical night. He danced as if he was possessed.

Now that he was beginning to get to know Jesus better and understood that there was a living God in heaven, he noticed that he sometimes found it less fun to dance these heathen dances. But even though he felt this way sometimes he just couldn't prevent himself from being drawn to the dancing once the drums started to beat.

One day, in connection with the Bible studies he was having with his neighbour, Mensah prayed his first prayer. He had decided to give his heart to the living God. He also wanted to live like a Christian. He wanted to learn to give Bible studies so that he could witness to others as his neighbour had done to him. Perhaps one day he would be able to get a better education at a Christian school, even become a pastor. He had great dreams and felt very happy.

Then Friday night came. The drums began to beat. Mensah tried not to listen, but the loud, frenzied drumming made itself heard through the cracks in his straw and mud house. In the end he couldn't resist the call of the drums, and before he really knew what he was doing he was part of the dance, forgetting everything else — until the drumming stopped. Then the spell was broken. Mensah went home and wept. How could he have denied his Lord after just a few days!

The next day, after he had talked to his Christian neighbour about the matter, they prayed together. Then the neighbour came up with an idea. 'I can help you. Every time the drums start to beat I shall come over to your house and we can talk and study the Bible together. It might be easier for you to withstand temptation if there are two of us.'

It worked perfectly. With the neighbour's help the temptation became less intense, and after a few weeks Mensah had overcome his compulsion to follow the drums.

PRAYER: Help me to be willing to support someone who is being tempted. Make me more aware of the problems and needs of others.

AN ENORMOUS CONSTRUCTION
For we are ... God's building.
1 CORINTHIANS 3:9

It took forty engineers and constructors two whole years to plan and prepare for the building of the Eiffel Tower in Paris. It took a further two years for several hundred builders and technicians to carry out the actual construction of the tower. It was completed in March 1889, and it was for many years the world's tallest building — 300 metres. There was no wonder it took such a long time to build and plan. It took, for example, five months to dig down to a depth of 15 metres on the side of the tower nearest the River Seine. This was to anchor the tower so that it wouldn't lean or move later on.

The four enormous arches which constitute the base of the tower take up about 8,094 square metres. These arches form the first platform of the tower which is about 60 metres above ground level. Every following platform becomes smaller and smaller in area. The last one is just a little platform with a flagpole and a lightning conductor.

The whole tower consists of 15,000 different types of wrought iron sections which were ready made at the iron foundry. The whole idea was that everything should be made ready for assembling at the building site. It meant lifting each part into place and riveting them together. Everything was made exactly according to the drawings, so exactly that not a single hole needed to be drilled again. Everything fitted perfectly. The 15,000 components were fastened together by 2,500,000 rivets.

Not only did the actual construction go smoothly and according to plan, but the tower has survived remarkably well for a hundred years. There has been hardly any need for repairs during this long period. Not a single rivet has needed to be replaced. What a skilful engineer Gustave Eiffel was!

PRAYER: Help me to plan my life in such a way that, with the Spirit's guidance, what I do will be what you can bless and will last. Spirit-led, help me to build a character which is strong enough to withstand all of life's strains and stresses.

MÜLLER NEEDS FOOD
And my God will meet all your needs according to his glorious riches in Christ Jesus.
PHILIPPIANS 4:19

The children had gone to bed. George Müller sat deep in thought. God had done so much for him before, but now there was a crisis. This is not to say that Müller was worried. He had learnt long ago to leave everything in God's hands. What he wondered about now was how God would produce enough food for breakfast for all the orphans he had in his children's home. There was literally nothing left to eat in the kitchen. The pantry was as empty as his purse. This was not unusual. Müller had often had the experience of receiving money just when he needed it and not before. That evening he prayed again for all the many children God had put under his care. He told the Lord that there was no breakfast for the morning. When he had talked things through with God he calmly went to bed.

The children in the home were blissfully ignorant of the fact that there was no breakfast for them next day. They woke up, washed, dressed, then went down and sat at the long tables in the dining room. The plates were in place, so were the spoons and cups. No one said anything about there being no food. The time came for the blessing to be said. George Müller prayed and thanked God for the food that was on its way, and then they all waited. The children, of course, thought that the food they were waiting for would come from the kitchen. The staff knew that if there was to be any food that day it would have to come from some other place. God had supported and helped Müller run his children's homes for several years. He had never had money to run such a big project — God had always sent ordinary people to help him with supplies or money just when they were needed. Now Müller waited again for God, the God who cared even more about these poor children than Müller did. And Müller wasn't to be disappointed this time either.

He had hardly finished saying the blessing when there was a knock on the door. There on the step stood the village baker. He explained quickly that God had woken him up in the night and asked him to get up at two o'clock to bake enough bread for all Müller's children. The baker carried in one big box of bread after another. It was more than enough for everyone. But God had still not finished with his answer to prayer. Before long there was another knock on the door. This time it was the milkman who stood there. He explained that his milk cart had broken down just outside the children's home. He wondered if the children could use all the milk he had with him because he couldn't pull his cart any further. Now the children had both bread and milk, just at the right time.

PRAYER: Lord, help me to trust you more and not worry about things which I can leave in your hands.

WHAT IS VALUABLE?

**"Do not store up for yourselves treasures on earth, where moth
and rust destroy, and where thieves break in and steal. But
store up for yourselves treasures in heaven . . . . For where your
treasure is, there your heart will be also."**
MATTHEW 6:19-21

Sometimes you can't help thinking what it would be like to own
a fortune. Then you could buy just what you wanted. You could
travel round the world. Or buy yourself a Rolls Royce. It would
seem that there is no limit to what you could do if you only
had the money.

You can easily be tempted to think that those who are fortunate
enough to be rich are happy, carefree people. However, some years
ago I got to know a lady who was a millionairess. Never have
I met a person who was so frightened, unhappy and anxious as
she was. I don't know how many doors she locked behind her
just to go down to empty the rubbish. If she was in town and
she heard fire engines, she would go rushing home in panic in
case it was her valuables that were burning. She often said, 'If
only you knew how difficult it is to be rich.' She really did sound
weighed down and depressed. I suggested once or twice that she
could give away part of what she owned to people who were
in need, thinking that she would then find her wealth less of a
burden. But she just wouldn't listen to suggestions like that. It
was as though she simply couldn't grasp such a concept, despite
the fact that she was a Christian.

There are certain things which cannot be bought for all the
money in the world. With money you can't, for example, buy inner
peace, true happiness or real friends. Nor can you always buy safety
and security.

When the war came to Burma, people began to flee. They quickly
packed together their valuables. The enemy was not going to get
a chance to lay his hands on these. However, the more gold and
valuables the fleeing people were trying to carry the harder the
journey became. These heavily-laden people could hardly keep
ahead of the enemy soldiers. Many of the rich then panicked. Those
who were travelling on foot called out in despair to the few who
had cars. They held out their hands full of gold and jewels in
the hope of buying themselves a seat in a vehicle in order to get
out of danger's way before it was too late. But their money was
of no use to them. In this tragic situation their gold was totally
valueless.

*PRAYER: Help me to understand that happiness is not found in money.
Help me to want to do something for others, even with the little I have,
so that I can have treasure in heaven — lasting treasure.*

POISON?

You guide me with your counsel.
PSALM 73:24

In a remote region of southern Ethiopia Margot had her tiny clinic where the sick could come for help. There was no doctor there, only Margot, a Swedish nurse who was trained in tropical medicine. All those whom she had helped loved her and called her 'Mamma Margot'. The clinic was small. It had only two rooms which could be used for in-patients. Usually the sick lived at home and came to visit the clinic regularly. Sometimes they were carried by relatives if they were unable to walk themselves.

One Thursday evening just before sundown a worried father came to the clinic. With him was his 14-year-old daughter who looked very ill indeed. The man explained agitatedly that his 5-year-old daughter had died the day before. Someone had put poison in her food, he said, and now his eldest daughter had also been poisoned. The father pleaded with Margot to save the girl's life. She examined the girl and found she had a high fever, but the father could perhaps be right and her illness had to do with poisoning. So Margot did what the father wanted and stomach-pumped the girl to get rid of the poison. There was no available bed at the clinic so the father took the girl home again and promised to come back with her the next day so that Nurse could take a look at her.

Friday came and went and they didn't return. This was not unusual. When patients felt they were better they didn't always return. Many other patients did come, however, and Margot was kept very busy and had little time to think of the poisoned girl. The next morning, Saturday, Margot noticed that her thoughts kept going to that sick girl. But no one came. Then Margot no longer just thought about the girl but felt a kind of compulsion to find her in her village. She took some medicine and a local woman who knew the area well. At last they found the right family. The girl was now really ill, running a temperature of over 40°C. She had not been poisoned but had a serious fever which would kill her in a few days if she were not given the correct medicine. Margot set to work on the very weak girl and a man from the family returned with her to the clinic to fetch the right medication. The girl received the tablets in time and her life was saved. Needless to say, Margot was glad that she had decided to go and check up on her patient.

PRAYER: God, give me a stronger faith in you and in your leading. Help me to go the extra mile.

THE PARDON

Give thanks to the Lord for he is good; his love endures for ever.
PSALM 118:1

Victoria became queen when she was barely 20 years old. She had to learn how to rule, and there were many things the young woman found difficult. Sometimes she just didn't know what to do for the best. So much depended on her that she sometimes felt the responsibility was almost too great to bear.

She had been queen for only a few months when she was visited at Windsor Castle by the Duke of Wellington. He had brought with him a whole pile of papers needing her signature. She read carefully through everything before she signed. Among the papers was one concerning a soldier who was condemned to death. If she signed the paper the man would be executed. She hesitated and began to question the Duke about him. The Duke explained that the man in question had committed several crimes and despite other punishments had not shown any willingness to become a better person. Queen Victoria sat in silence for some time and then asked the Duke if he could say anything positive about this soldier. Had he never done anything for which he could be praised? Yes, he had, the Duke explained. This soldier had, on repeated occasions, shown himself to be both brave and patriotic. The Queen sat deep in thought again. Finally she decided what she would do.

She asked the Duke to visit the soldier in prison and show him the document condemning him to death, under which she now wrote the word 'Pardoned'. She asked the Duke to explain to the soldier that she had pardoned him because she had heard that he was brave and courageous. She also asked the Duke to keep her informed as to what happened to the pardoned soldier.

The Queen's wish was respected. The soldier was told what her majesty had said and done. He was deeply moved by the thought that the young Queen had intervened and saved his life despite the way he had been living. He decided that from then on he would be the best and most faithful soldier in the Queen's army. And that's just what he became. When he returned to civilian life a few years later he continued to be thankful for the pardon he had been given and his exemplary life reflected his gratitude.

PRAYER: Lord, you who are the King of kings, thank you for the forgiveness which you so willingly give us in your great love, and the encouragement it give us to try again.

THE BREAKDOWN

**Do not withhold good from those who deserve it, when
it is in your power to act.**
PROVERBS 3:27

When I was a teacher in Ghana another girl and I went on
a trip. We took her little car and travelled the long distance
to northern Ghana and a little way into Upper Volta. It was
an exciting trip, way out beyond the reaches of civilization. We
met about one car a day on those dusty, pot-holed roads. After
five days of this her old Volkswagen had had enough and went
on strike. We knew no more about cars than that the VW had
its engine in the back!

So there we sat out on the savannah in the heat of the midday
sun, miles away from the nearest village and even further away
from drinking water. There was little hope that anyone would
pass by. After some hours, when we had begun to feel ill from
sitting in the hot sun, a car came past. After we had persuaded
the driver to stop we found that he was a Russian. His daughter
was travelling with him. They kindly took a look at our engine
and then the man said in broken English, 'Do not drive car
— it explode.' Then he drove off and left us!

On the verge of despair we kept waiting in the hope that
someone else would pass. After some time we heard another
car approaching which we stopped. This time it was two Italians
with a Ghanaian driver. They too looked at the motor and said
in broken English, 'Not drive this car — it explode.' Then they
went and sat in their car. We prayed quietly to God that these
people would not also leave us there. They talked together for
a while and then started looking for a rope to tow us with.
They found none in their car and in ours we found something
which was a cross between string and thin rope. We tied it
on doubled in order to make it strong enough. The drawback
with this was that by then the rope was no longer than 150cm
which brought us very close to the car in front. To make matters
worse the first car was driven by the Ghanaian driver who kept
to his usual speed of around 100km an hour.

After several frightening emergency stops to avoid running over
goats or people sitting or lying on the usually quiet road, the
'rope' had to be retied. In the end there was only about half
a metre between the towing car and us. After six hair-raising
hours of driving we arrived at the nearest town, exhausted but
very thankful.

When we offered to pay the Italians for all the trouble they
had taken they refused to take a single penny. When we said
again how fortunate it was that they had come along at a time

when we needed help so badly they answered: 'It was not fortunate, it was the God in heaven. He led us.' That's how we felt about it too.

PRAYER: Lord, lead me today to someone who needs my help.

THE INDIAN CHIEF

"If your enemy is hungry, feed him; if he is thirsty, give him something to drink . . . ." Do not be overcome by evil; but overcome evil by good.
ROMANS 12:20, 21

The settlers along the frontier in North America often experienced attacks from Indians who wanted to move them out of the area. Sometimes the Indians' attacks became so violent that the government had to intervene by force to restore law and order. In such cases troops were sent out to put things right. This was usually easier said than done. The Indians wouldn't surrender without a struggle. On one such occasion the result of the action was that sixty Indians were taken captive. They were put under arrest in a military outpost called Fort Marion. The commanding officer, Captain Pratt, soon realized that violence got him nowhere with these Indians whom he thought were fine people. He decided to try to win their trust by love instead. His aim was to help both red and white to live together without fighting.

It was relatively easy for him to get in contact with quite a number of the Indians and to become their friend. However, the Indian chief refused to accept Captain Pratt's kindness and remained disagreeable and obstinate. The Captain did all in his power to win the friendship of this tall and stately chief. Nothing helped. The chief remained just as sullen and aggressive. One day he took the chief with him on a walk. When they returned to the fort it was late in the evening, so Captain Pratt took the Indian chief home to his house instead. He showed him the guest room and gave him a nice soft bed to sleep on and locked the door. The next morning the Captain invited the chief to sit next to him at the table. They were going to have porridge as usual, but the chief refused to touch it and sat there obstinately. Mrs. Pratt thought that perhaps the chief didn't like porridge. She promised at once to make him his favourite food if only he would eat with them.

When the proud old warrior heard this his facial expression changed and he seemed moved. He rose from the table and the family wondered what would happen next. Suddenly the chief burst into tears. He explained that there was nothing wrong with the porridge, but that he was humbled by their kindness. 'I was your enemy. I would have killed you if I had had the chance. But you invite me to your home and let me sit at your table like an old friend. I cannot eat with you until I have shaken your hand to show that I have made peace with you'. He then went up to each member of the family and took their hand. After that he was a changed man. He became friendly, open and willing to co-operate.

PRAYER: Lord, show me how to be kind, even to those who have hurt me.

MISTRUSTED

May the words of my mouth and the meditation of my heart be pleasing in your sight, O Lord, my Rock and my Redeemer.
PSALM 19:14

In the middle of the 60s I was a teacher at a boarding school in Ghana. There were about 400 students aged between 16 and 40. At that time the country was as good as bankrupt. The government and the business community had no money to buy food from abroad, and what could be produced within the country was soon consumed by the large population. The more difficult the food situation became the more time the principal had to spend driving round from one town to another in an attempt to secure enough rice, cassava and flour for the school kitchen.

One evening when he had been away for three days in an effort to find food for the school, there were about 100 adult male students waiting for him on the school's car park. 'That was kind of them', he thought, tired as he was. The students crowded round the little lorry to see what the principal had bought. At that particular point in time the students had been without margarine for a couple of weeks, which was something they did not appreciate. The principal had spent three days trying to get hold of margarine, but there just wasn't any to be had. When he explained this to the students they became furious. They tried to turn the little lorry over, they ran round shouting and became more and more aggressive. They accused him of giving the margarine to the staff members instead of to the students.

The principal, who loved his students and had worked in Africa for many years, actually cried. As he put it, 'I have done all I can for these people and they still don't trust me. It hurts so much.'

When I saw him suffer that evening it made me think of how Jesus must have felt when time and again he was misunderstood and misinterpreted. The people he came to help turned their backs on him. Have you ever thought that when you say, 'I don't care   65 about Jesus', or 'Jesus doesn't care about me. If he did he would help me with this or that', you are actually hurting the one who loves you more than anyone else does, and who plans everything for your best.

PRAYER: Lord, thank you for loving me. Help me to trust that you want the best for me, and help me not to hurt you today.

LAMBARÉNÉ

"Go into all the world and preach the good news to all creation."
MARK 16:15

What do you do with your life when you are gifted in several areas? How do you choose which gift to concentrate on? Young Albert asked himself such questions. He loved music and played the organ very well. He also composed beautiful organ music. He loved reading and wrote books. Should he become a musician or a writer? While he was wondering about his future he continued his studies at the university and when he was 26 years old he received his doctorate in three subjects, philosophy, theology and music. Now he had even more choices for his future profession. How should he plan?

He worked for some time as a curate and organist in his homeland of Switzerland. A few years passed and then this gifted man became sure of what God wanted him to do with his life — he developed a real longing to become a missionary in Africa. People thought he had gone mad. What was he to do out in the jungle with his high education? Wasn't that a way of wasting all the talents God had given him? But Albert was sure. By this time he was 30 and had begun to study medicine. He was forced to work to support himself while he studied, and it took him eight years to finish medical school.

He was finally ready to go to Africa and pass on to others the joy of life he felt. He went to Gabon, and with his own hands built up a hospital where he was both doctor and priest. The hospital grew with the years and soon resembled a large village. Here families with sick relatives could come and live. Out there, miles away from civilization, he worked night and day, and experienced real happiness. The only luxury he allowed himself was a simple organ. In the evenings, whenever he had a spare moment, he would sit and play. He continued to write books. He was a man always on the go.

Albert Schweitzer spent the rest of his life in this little place out in the middle of nowhere. His mission station was called

Lambaréné, and many Europeans visited it to learn how to help people in the Third World. Out there among the sick and poor, Schweitzer experienced a life that was meaningful and worth living. This famous man received the Nobel Peace Prize in 1952.

PRAYER: Lord, show me your plan for my life. I would like to show my thankfulness to you for all you do for me.

THE POEM

Christ, in whom are hidden all the treasures of
wisdom and knowledge.
COLOSSIANS 2:2, 3

Tomorrow was the day of the big exam in English Literature. Mary had studied hard in preparation for several months now. This was the last big exam she would face at university, and covered the literary works of many different authors. It also dealt with around a thousand poems by many poets.

Mary had prayed about her studies during the years she had been at university, had many times experienced that God helped her and was interested in her studies. Now, the evening before the exam, she sat on the floor and looked at the piles of books stacked there, books she would be questioned on in the morning. She tried to guess what the professor would ask her about, and what she should have one last look at. It was impossible to read through everything. She decided it was best to leave it in God's hands. She had studied hard all term and done her part.

As she sat there on the floor thinking, she noticed a collection of poems which she had read at the start of the term. She didn't remember much about them other than that the poems were short and about Christian subjects. Why not read a few of those before she went to bed? A kind of evening worship. She eyed through several pages and paused at a poem called *The Collar*. She mused on the strange title. Why was it called that? She quickly read through the poem, but it was hard to see how it related to the title. It said nothing about collars. It spoke instead of how a person who was trying to run away from God, felt himself drawn back to God all the time because of Jesus' love. Strange. She read the poem once more. Could it be that the love of Jesus acted as a kind of collar and leash which pulled a person slowly but surely back to God? She shut the book and went to bed.

The next day at the oral exam a question was asked about one poem out of the thousand on the list. The very one she had thought so much about the evening before. The question was: 'Why is this poem called *The Collar*?' That was just 67 what she had wondered about. The answer she had worked out the previous night was also the correct one. She was amazed to think that God, who has so much else of importance to do, even cares about a student's studies!

PRAYER: You who are all Wisdom, thank you for caring about our education, and for being willing to give us the ability to learn and remember.

THE CONVICT

Then I acknowledged my sin to you and did not cover up my iniquity. I said, "I will confess my transgressions to the Lord" — and you forgave the guilt of my sin.
PSALM 32:5

The Spanish Duke of Osuna was on his way down to the harbour in Barcelona. Several galleons were docked there, manned mostly by convicts. Instead of sitting in a prison cell these men were forced to work on the ship, often having to row the large boats when there was no wind. They had to work under whip lashes and were treated worse than slaves. But it was impossible to escape as they were chained to the ship when they were in or near a port.

The Duke was going to inspect his vessels. He was in a good mood that day and decided that he would do something for one of the convicts. On one particular ship he had the convicts brought up on deck and went round and spoke to them all to find out what they had done to be in that position. Most of the normally sullen men were very keen to speak now that they had the chance. It appeared that no one had done anything wrong. It was always someone else's fault that the man had been convicted. And how they complained about the way they were being treated!

However, the Duke knew that the men were lying. Many of them were convicted of murder or robbery with violence. No one would admit it, though. Perhaps they thought that by playing innocent the Duke would want to pardon them and let them go free. But the Duke saw through them.

He had just about lost all desire to do anything for anyone when he came across a convict who behaved quite differently. When the Duke asked him what he had done he explained humbly that he had been caught stealing and that he was being justly punished for a crime of which he sorely repented. He explained that it was his own fault that he was a slave on the ship. He seemed to feel that by all the hard work he was making up for his wrong action. The Duke looked at the repentant man and told him that from
68 now on he would be a free man, pardoned. The Duke explained

to the rest of the crew that as they had done nothing wrong there was nothing he could pardon them for! He didn't want to free anyone who was not willing to repent of his crime, or he would just go out and repeat his former mistakes.

PRAYER: Thank you, Lord, that you forgive us so willingly when we confess our sins, freeing us from the slavery it brings.

I UNDERSTAND EVERYTHING YOU SAID

Utterly amazed, they asked: "Are not all these men who are speaking Galileans? Then how is it that each of us hears them in his own native language?"
ACTS 2:7, 8

There are parts of Finland where the local people speak only Swedish, a language quite unrelated to Finnish. In one such area a Swedish evangelist was holding a series of meetings. He knew no Finnish. Quite a lot of people came to hear him speak and after every meeting he went to the back of the hall to talk to the visitors, get to know them a little, and give them a chance to ask questions.

After a few weeks he knew most of the people who came to the meetings. He was able to look out over his congregation to see if there was anyone he had missed. Yes, there was a lady sitting near the front, always in the same place, wearing the same coat and hat. How could he have forgotten her? She was always so deeply attentive and seemed to be touched by the message he preached. The evangelist remembered that she usually left during the last hymn, as if she had a bus to catch.

He was anxious to get a chance to meet this lady who seemed so interested in the Bible. He decided to go down from the platform during the last hymn in order to greet her before she disappeared. For several weeks she managed to get out ahead of him. Now the series of meetings was nearly over. Several people had already spoken with him about wanting to give their hearts to the Lord. He wondered sometimes what this interested lady was thinking. Had she decided to follow her Lord too? He still had not shaken hands with her. She had always gone out just before he arrived at the door.

The last night but one she remained behind and went up to him and began to speak. He was glad to meet her at last, but was very surprised when she addressed him in Finnish, a language he couldn't understand at all. He told her in Swedish that he didn't know any Finnish and couldn't understand what she said. She 69 looked quite confused, and continued to talk in Finnish. It was impossible to communicate. In the end the pastor had to ask one of his helpers who was bilingual to come and help him out. Not till then did the pastor really understand that this woman was Finnish and that she could neither speak nor understand Swedish. But she had understood all he had said in the meetings! He questioned her to check this. She had heard him speak Finnish! And now she wanted him to know she had given her heart to the Lord.

PRAYER: Thank you, Lord, that today, as in the days of the apostles, you can still reach all those who want to hear about you.

STARTING AGAIN FROM SCRATCH

He who began a good work in you will carry it on to completion until the day of Christ Jesus.
PHILIPPIANS 1:6

For many years Albert had looked forward to the day when he would finish his medical studies and start work as a missionary in Africa. At last the great day came. He had worked hard to earn enough money for the long journey to Africa and for all the medicines and equipment he needed to take with him. Things he wouldn't be able to buy there. Now he would soon be in the mission hospital that a missionary society had promised to build for him.

When he and his wife arrived at the designated place, far out in the jungle, they had an unpleasant surprise. There were no buildings at all, let alone a hospital! Albert was disappointed but set about making a little clinic so that the sick could be helped. Nearby he found a hen-house which he cleaned out with the help of some of the local people, putting up shelves for his medicines. Then he put a camp bed in the middle of the floor to serve as an operating table. He was ready for the patients to come, and they did, in a steady stream. In this simple hen-house he performed operations, saving lives and treating all who needed help.

With so many patients he soon needed a larger building, so at the same time as he treated his patients he organized the work of building a proper hospital. The floor was made of cement and the walls and roof of corrugated iron. Albert and his wife, who was a nurse, didn't have chance to use this building for more than a few months before the First World War broke out and, being German, they were forced to return to Europe as prisoners. Five years later when the war was over Albert Schweitzer and his wife were tired and sick. It took a couple of years before he recovered his health and had saved up enough money to return to his beloved Africa.

When he came back to his little hospital everything had been spoiled by termites, damp and heat. But Albert didn't give up. He started again from the beginning, at the same time caring for the long lines of patients. With the help of local people there was soon a simple hospital on the spot. After a few years he had a 300-bed hospital.

Albert Schweitzer, the missionary, the doctor, became famous and his work continued to grow as help came in from many sources. Despite all the attention he received he remained a humble man who lived out his love to God by helping others.

PRAYER: Dear God, give me the courage to start again when things have gone wrong.

WHERE'S THE SHOP?

"I am the Lord your God, who teaches you what is best for you, who directs you in the way you should go."
ISAIAH 48:17

Rosemary looked at her watch. One and a half hours till the bus left. She had finished her shopping and been in the library for quite a while. What to do next to pass the time? Then she remembered the religious book shop. She knew the lady who worked there and had often been in and talked to her. She would do that now. It was too cold to stand around and wait.

She set off towards the shop which wasn't far from the bus station. The town centre was not large and she knew it well. She walked for quite a while not thinking of anything in particular. Then someone came past on a bike and stopped her. It was a lady who sang in the same choir as she did. They began to talk and it soon became obvious that she was very worried. Perplexed, confused and depressed, she didn't know what God wanted her to do to solve a number of serious problems. As Rosemary talked to her, telling her how God is happy to help, and gave her some ideas as to what she could do, the lady began to look less tense.

After a while a gentleman they both knew came along and asked them what they were doing in this part of the town. The lady answered first: 'I came cycling along and saw Rosemary and stopped to talk because I felt so depressed and worried. But I feel much better. I know that God can help me solve my problems now.' The man turned to Rosemary and asked her what *she* was doing in that part of town. Rosemary turned round 71 and pointed up the street. 'I was on my way to the religious book shop . . .' Then she stopped and stared in the direction she was pointing. She turned round to get her bearings. Where *was* she, anyway? This was a completely different street. There was no bookshop here. How could she have made such a mistake in a town she knew so well?

Could it be that the Lord wanted her to meet a discouraged woman to whom she could give new courage and a stronger faith in God? It certainly seemed like it!

PRAYER: Lord, if there is someone I can encourage today, lead me to that person.

STOP A WHILE

Praise the Lord, O my soul . . . he redeems my life from the pit.
PSALM 103:2, 4

Sarah loved driving her car. She got such pleasure out of watching the landscape change as she drove; farms, woods, villages and old churches. There was always something interesting to look at which made long, lonely journeys pass quickly. On this particular day she was out driving some distance away in an area that was new to her. It's nice to see new places, she thought as she drove along. She was just going up a steep incline when she thought she heard someone speak to her, though she knew she was on her own. She listened, but couldn't quite understand what had been said.

When she had just about reached the top of the hill she understood enough to realize that she ought to pull over to the side of the road and stop the car. She felt rather strange doing so, but she had plenty of time and was curious as to what it could mean, so she stopped the car at the top of the hill. She parked in a layby so that she would not be in the way if someone wanted to pass. Then she sat and waited. Was it God's voice she had heard, or was it just an idea she'd had? If so, where had the idea come from? She wan't feeling tired, so rest was not what she needed. As she sat there she heard a vehicle coming from the opposite direction. She couldn't see what it was because there was a sharp bend on the top of the hill. It must be something big, though, because it was making an awful noise. Suddenly it was right in front of her. It was a long lorry with a trailer, but it wasn't progressing as it should. For some reason the driver had temporarily lost control of the heavy vehicle and it was swaying and skidding on the wrong side of the road, the side that Sarah would have been on if she had continued. Her heart was in her mouth as the lorry lurched past, coming so close that she could have reached out and touched it.

Her little car would have been smashed completely if she had been out there on the road. It was obvious that it had not been her own fantasy that had made her pull in. It was God's voice which had spoken and saved her life. Once she had calmed down she continued her journey, praising God and thanking him for caring.

PRAYER: *Gracious Lord, be with me today and protect me from danger.*

THE OTHER CHEEK

"If someone strikes you on one cheek, turn to him the other also."
LUKE 6:29

Daniel lived in East Africa a number of years ago. He attended a Christian school for several years and, despite the fact that his father was a witch-doctor and very much against Christianity, Daniel decided to be baptized and belong to Jesus. It was not always easy for him to live as a Christian, particularly not during the school holidays when he was home with his family who all worshipped evil spirits and home-made idols. Daniel was often teased, but by praying to God for help he succeeded in keeping calm.

Daniel's home was a long way away from the boarding school he attended. His family didn't have much money, hence he was often forced to walk that long distance. It took several days either way. On one occasion when he was on his way back to school after a holiday he got the idea that he could take a short cut and perhaps save up to an hour's walking. It was worth a try. He was hot and the sun's heat was merciless. Anything to save a bit of time. He would need to pass over the property of another school where all the staff were Europeans. There were no signs saying not to pass that way, so Daniel thought that if he kept to the paths no damage would be done.

He hadn't gone more than halfway across the area when he met a very angry European who asked him sharply what he was doing on private ground. Daniel explained honestly and kindly that he was on his way to school and that he had taken a short cut. The man looked at him with distrust. He was sure he was on his way to the hen-house to steal eggs. Eggs had been disappearing for the last few days. This young man must be a thief. The man shouted at Daniel and hit him hard across one ear. Daniel was taken by surprise. He hadn't done anything to deserve this. But he had learned not to retaliate. All was quiet for a moment, and then Daniel did what Jesus said we should do when hit. He turned his other cheek towards the man, kindly but decidedly.

The man, who was on the point of giving the supposed thief 73 a thrashing, let his hand drop. He had also read that text. Here stood a young African who lived according to what the Bible taught while he himself didn't even try. The man's eyes filled with tears and he apologized to Daniel for the way he had behaved, and asked him more about the school he attended, keeping him company for a while as he walked on his way.

PRAYER: Lord, help me not to 'pay people back' when they hurt me, but to show kindness to them instead.

THE TWINS

"We have found the one . . . about whom the prophets also wrote — Jesus of Nazareth."
JOHN 1:45

As regards looks they were like two peas in a pod, with pretty round faces, a twinkle in the eye, and a smile that usually played around their lips. They were identical (one-egg) twins and it was probably only their parents who could be sure which was which. The only difference I could find with the two teenage girls was that one of them had a small brown birthmark on her neck, but you can't always manage to check that before you greet them!

Yvonne and Carina shared everything and did everything together. They both had the same girl-friend in school, a girl the same age called Ann-Christine. She went round with the twins and had in that way two friends rolled into one. But Ann-Christine received something more than just the friendship of a pair of twins. Yvonne and Carina were Christians and though they were still young they dared to talk about their faith. Sometimes they invited their friend to their church when there was something special on.

The three stayed together even during their early teens. When it came time to do their 'A' levels they chose different courses and ended up at different schools, but they still met in their spare time. Then one spring there was going to be a big evangelistic campaign in the twins' church. They invited their friend Ann-Christine to come and listen. She did so and began to think deeply about what was being said. At the end of the series of meetings she decided she wanted to give her heart to the Lord. The twins were overjoyed.

It wasn't long, however, before the three girls were in for a real shock. Ann-Christine's mother refused to hear of her daughter being baptized, and said that if she went ahead with this plan she would no longer be allowed to live at home. What 74 was Ann-Christine to do? She still hadn't finished her 'A' levels and could not support herself. Nor did she want to hurt her mother. She prayed very much about this painful situation and was soon convinced that if she put Christ first in her life God would arrange all the rest for her. She was baptized and as a result forced to move away from home. But after only a few weeks her mother welcomed her back home again.

Today Ann-Christine is studying to become a church worker. All because the twins were not too shy to talk about their faith and invite their friend to church.

PRAYER: God, give me more courage to witness to my friends and to dare to invite them to church.

ABLE TO ANSWER

"When you are brought before ... authorities, do not worry about how you will defend yourselves or what you will say."
LUKE 12:11

Alice sat outside the door and waited. Soon it would be her turn to go in. Her heart was beating fast and her knees were knocking. She was 19, shy, and had always found oral questions hard to answer. And now she was going to be asked masses of questions. So much depended on the outcome of this interview. She prayed for help. God was the only one she could take into the room with her.

Now the questioning had started. She sat there, tense, and answered as well as she could the questions about her studies and practical knowledge. The five people who were firing the questions at her were to decide whether she was suitable for sending out as a Voluntary Service Overseas teacher to a school in Africa. They weighed every word she said. Sometimes there were long pauses while they thought and pondered.

On the application form Alice had filled in, there were several questions about her church affiliation and faith. The five who were trying her case were not connected to any church organization. After a while they began to ask her how a Christian would behave in Africa under certain very unusual circumstances. They gave examples. Alice found it hard to work out quick answers to these tricky questions and began to panic. She desperately wanted to be accepted as a volunteer teacher and be able to go to Africa. She also wanted to explain to these five people how a Christian reacts in everyday situations as well as in moments of crisis, but she just couldn't get a word out.

She sent up a silent call to God for help. To her great surprise she noticed that suddenly she could speak clearly and that those who were questioning her sat listening intently. It seemed to Alice that she too was sitting back and listening. The words and thoughts seemed to come from someone other than herself. This remarkable situation continued for about ten minutes, the period of time the interview dealt with religious matters. When the questions reverted to practical things Alice was just as nervous and found it just as hard to think as before. All her tension and nerves had come back again.

To her great joy Alice was selected among many who had applied for work as teachers in the Third World. If you ask Alice what she thinks about today's text she will tell you that she herself has experienced a little of this wonderful promise of help from Jesus.

PRAYER: Thank you, Lord for your promise of wisdom and help when we find ourselves in situations where we need to explain what you mean to us.

A FRIEND CAN MEAN SO MUCH

Perfume and incense bring joy to the heart, and the pleasantness of one's friend springs from his earnest counsel.
PROVERBS 27:9

David was a Scotsman, short, tough and very persistent. He was born near Glasgow in 1813. His parents were poor and David was forced to start working at the cotton mill while he was still a child. Despite the fact that he worked a fourteen-hour day at the mill he spent the evenings studying and eventually qualified as a medical doctor.

When he was 27 he travelled out to what was then a dangerous and unknown continent — Africa. Once there he worked as a missionary, as a doctor, an opponent of the slave trade, an explorer and a master builder. He radiated such love to others that he could pass through dangerous areas where not even armed soldiers dared show themselves. The local people loved this small hard-working man.

With the passing of the years exploration became his main task. He set off on his last journey in 1866, together with thirty-six bearers and helpers. During this journey many of the men became sick and died. David Livingstone himself fell ill, having contracted several serious tropical illnesses at once. Everything seemed to have gone wrong. So when some of his remaining bearers ran off, taking with them his stock of medicine, it was like a death blow to him. By 1871 he had nothing left at all, and he was completely alone and very ill. All hope seemed to have gone.

Meanwhile, back in the West, David Livingstone had become

a famous man, and many people in Europe and America were interested in him, but no one knew where he was or if he was still alive. An American newspaper sent out a reporter to try to find Livingstone. The reporter's name was Henry Morton Stanley. After many long months of hardship and searching he finally found the sick man, way out in the bush in a little hut. Stanley had medicines with him, good food, news from the wide world, but above all, friendship. As a result of Stanley's friendship and care, Livingstone received new courage and regained his desire to travel further in an effort to find the source of the Nile. Stanley's visit, which lasted only a few months, gave Livingstone so much inner strength and warmth that he continued to explore the unknown continent of Africa for another year before he died. Stanley was the last westerner Livingstone saw.

PRAYER: Lord, teach me how I can spread hope and courage to those who are sad and down.

A STRANGE FLEET

**I am not seeking my own good but the good of many,
so that they may be saved.**
1 CORINTHIANS 10:33

The word was quietly spread round the south coast of England: 'Winnie needs boats.' Winnie was the nickname for Sir Winston Churchill and the time was May 1940 during the Second World War. Churchill had led the British resistance to Hitler's advances in Europe. He had organized an attack against the Germans who had invaded France, but the whole thing had failed and the British and French armies were on the retreat. Now they were down on the beaches at Dunkirk. If they were not helped off the beaches the whole force faced certain death.

That is why the message was whispered round the coast: 'Winnie needs boats.' All the naval vessels were already engaged in various areas and now there was no time to wait for them to return. The only hope for the troops marooned on the beaches were ordinary, privately owned boats. Most of the men in England were already conscripted and those who were left along the coasts were teachers, doctors, dentists, farmers, fishermen, pensioners and youth who were not yet 18. Churchill set about co-ordinating the use of these men and about 850 small boats which had been found, mostly boats not built to go across open sea. There were, of course, many fishing boats and some cruisers. Many of the others were sailing boats, barges, tugs and motorboats. These small craft were to be manned by dentists, bank 77

managers and youth — even pensioners. These relatively un-
trained men took what they had on hand in the way of boats.
Detailed plans were laid for what was secretly known as 'Oper-
ation Dynamo'.

On 27 May they set off from Britain. When this 'toy' fleet
came into sight the stranded soldiers were overjoyed and waded
out to meet their rescuers. Can you believe it, but this tiny
fleet, working a shuttle service from 27 May to 3 June, managed
to evacuate 200,000 British soldiers! Not only that, they were
even able to take with them 140,000 French soldiers too! The
whole thing becomes even more incredible when you remember
that this amateur fleet was under continuous fire. Admittedly
the weather conditions were perfect. The sea was calm and the
sky heavily overcast which made things difficult for the German
planes as they tried to stop the tiny boats.

This is an example of what happens when you take the available resources and get on with the job, rather than sitting down
and fretting because you do not have the proper things you
think you need.

*PRAYER: Lord, help me to help others with the little I have. Make me
an instrument for saving someone for you.*

SINGLE-HANDED ROUND THE WORLD

**Forgetting what is behind and straining towards what is ahead,
I press on towards the goal to win the prize for which God has
called me heavenwards in Christ Jesus. All of us who are
mature should take such a view of things.**
PHILIPPIANS 3:13-15

The beacons were lit on the hills of Devon round Plymouth harbour. The year was 1967. These beacons had been used in earlier
times over a period of many hundreds of years to signal that important ships were on their way into the harbour. The beacons
had been lit nearly four hundred years before, for example, when
Sir Francis Drake sailed into Plymouth. But now it was May 1967
and the same beacons were lit to announce that a boat was on its
way into port. The boat in question was a very small one, a sailing
boat only 16 metres long, being managed by just one man. Why
was this boat so remarkable that the beacons should be lit and
a quarter of a million people gather near the harbour in Plymouth
to welcome it?

The boat was called *Gypsy Moth*, and wasn't very unusual. But
the man who sailed her *was*. His name was Francis Chichester,
and when he sailed into Plymouth on 28 May he had just com-

pleted a round-the-world trip in his tiny boat, all on his own. No small achievement for one man in a boat which lacked any form of motor, wholly dependent on the winds.

But the whole thing becomes even more remarkable when you find out more about Chichester himself. At the time of his round-the-world voyage he was a pensioner, or at least became one during the trip. He actually had his 65th birthday out in the middle of the Atlantic! Chichester had been very ill for several years before he set off on his great adventure. He was suffering from lung cancer which made him very weak. His eyesight was also bad. However, he was a man who was not going to give up easily. He wanted to fight till the last.

It took him 107 days to reach Sydney, Australia, the end of the first stage of his journey round the world. He had to rest there for a month because he was so weak when he arrived that he could hardly walk. Once he felt rested and some repairs and altera-tions had been made to the boat, he was off again. This time it took him 116 days of struggling to get back to Plymouth in the other direction. He had hoped to sail faster and break a record. He always aimed high. Even if he was old and sick he was going to do his very best to the very end.

PRAYER: Lord, give me the courage to keep up the struggle when every-thing seems hopeless. I want to reach the goal you have set for me — salvation and eternal life.

JOHN THE SALESMAN

**Now an angel . . . said to Philip, "Go south to the road —
the desert road — that goes down from Jerusalem
to Gaza." So he started out.**
ACTS 8:26, 27

John was from India. He was a Christian, and in order to earn enough for his college fees so that he could study to become a pastor, he worked in Sweden during the summer selling Christian literature. He went from door to door, demonstrating his books, hoping that people would want to buy them. In his bag he had books for both children and adults — on the Bible and on health subjects.

One day as he was out canvassing on the outskirts of a small town called Kalmar, it seemed as if no one wanted to buy any-thing from him. He had worked for several hours and only had 'no' for an answer. He felt impressed that he should get on his moped and drive off in a certain direction. Since everything had gone so badly, he thought he might as well try out the idea.

He started to drive in that direction. Soon the houses finished 79 and the woods started. How strange, he thought. What was he supposed to do out there if there were no houses? However, he decided to drive on a bit further along the road. He soon came to a fork in the road. He stopped his moped and took a look around. The road to the right had quite a few houses along it, whereas to the left there were only two houses. John decided to go down the right fork as he felt he would have a better chance of selling his books there. But as he started to drive in that direction he felt strongly that he should go to the left instead. So he turned down the left fork and drove slowly towards the two houses. Two ladies were standing in the garden of the first house, talking together. John decided to drive past that first house. The ladies were sure to say 'No thank you' before he had even opened his bag. But as he began to drive past the house he felt impressed that this was the house he was to visit.

He stopped his moped and went up the path with his bagful of books. One of the ladies had gone by now, but the other one listened politely while he told her about his books. When he had shown her all the different books he had in his bag she looked disappointed and said, 'Haven't you got anything else with you? No Bible story books?' 'Yes', he had, 'in the other bag that is still on the moped.' He went to fetch it and when he showed her the books she said, 'For the past five years I have been praying that I would be able to get hold of these books. I had seen them at a friend's house and have waited all this time to buy a set for myself.' Then John knew why he had been impressed to drive out into the woods. God wanted him to be part of an answer to prayer.

PRAYER: Lord, make me more aware of your voice. May I be willing to be led to someone who needs my help.

THE LIFE LINE

This is how God showed his love among us: He sent his one and only Son into the world that we might live through him.
1 JOHN 4:9

One day as I was walking along the coast near the mouth of a large river in the north of Sweden, I saw something strange out in the water. It seemed to be some sort of marker and next to it there was a dark object in the water. I made my way closer in order to see what it was. The dark object turned out to be the head of a man swimming. By this time I had noticed, to my surprise, that there were quite a few men out in the cold water, each one swimming or floating next to the marker. They didn't seem in any danger and behaved calmly, as though there was some purpose for their being there. I decided to sit down in the grass and watch what happened.

Before long each of the men had stopped swimming and was lying on a dark inflatable raft just big enough for one. I watched them climb up onto these and then lay back and rest. It looked very strange to see six men bobbing up and down on the small wavelets of the river mouth. What were they waiting for?

After what seemed to me a long wait, I heard the sound of powerful rotor blades and a large military helicopter appeared. Slowly it made its way to the area where the men lay waiting on their rubber rafts. Now things began to get really interesting. The helicopter went down low over the water and the big side doors were opened. Inside I could see several men working on something which looked like a long rope with a harness. I came to the conclusion that the point of all this was to 'save' the men in the water by winching them up into the helicopter. It was a sea rescue practice for those doing their military service. I wondered how they would set about the rescue. It was hard to see exactly what was going on inside the hovering helicopter. Finally things seemed to be ready and a strong life-line was let down. To my surprise it was not just a life-line. Hooked on to the line was not only a harness — there was also a man!

With some precision flying by the pilot the man on the end of the life-line hung exactly above one of the men in the water. Once in position he was slowly lowered down to the level of the raft. There the man on the end of the line fixed a second harness on to the man on the raft. When things were properly fastened he gave a signal to the helicopter and the two men were slowly winched up to safety. This manoeuvre was repeated until all six men in the water were picked up.

PRAYER: Thank you, Jesus, that you came down to earth yourself to save us and didn't just send a life-line.

THE CRASH

The eyes of the Lord are on those who fear him, on those whose hope is in his unfailing love, to deliver them from death.
PSALM 33:18, 19

The African pastor looked at the speedometer. It showed about 120km an hour on the steep downhill drive. The heavily-loaded bus — a kind of remodelled lorry — began to sway. The driver, who was clearly under the influence of alcohol, seemed completely unaware of the dangerous situation. The pastor realized, however, and was fully aware that an accident was about to happen. He knew this particular mud road well, so that even though it was 81 now pitch dark outside he knew they would soon reach the point where there were several sharp bends.

The pastor was in charge of the churches in a number of the larger villages. He had no car of his own and when he was to preach in any of the villages he was forced to go by public transport — lorry-buses. Unfortunately it happened quite often that he had to travel with drivers who were drunk, but the man who drove today was so much under the influence of palm wine that he had no understanding of what he was doing.

The pastor called to God for help as the lorry increased in speed, careering down the hillside. Suddenly the pastor found that he was no longer in the bus. He found himself walking on the road close to where the village began. With a thankful heart filled with wonder, he made his way to the small clay church where he was to preach. He hadn't quite reached the building when a car came from the same direction. The driver called out to the villagers that a serious accident had taken place where the road bent sharply on the steep downhill section. It appeared that all those in the bus had been killed. The people began to talk about the accident and speculate on who could have been among the passengers. The pastor listened for a while then said, 'I know, I was on that lorry.' Everyone stopped talking and stared at him, anxious to know what he meant. When he tried to explain what had happened the people wanted to know more about how God had saved him from certain death. There were more than usual in his congregation that night to hear him preach, and they kept on coming to hear him whenever he visited the village. Here was a man who had a living God.

PRAYER: Lord, when I am frightened or discouraged remind me that there is nothing you cannot handle. Help me to rely on you.

THE TRAIN JOURNEY

God has said, "Never will I leave you; never will I forsake you." So we say with confidence, "The Lord is my helper; I will not be afraid."
HEBREWS 13:5, 6

One summer in the 60s I travelled by train in France and Switzerland with Angela whom I like to call my foster sister. One day we visited Locarno, a pretty town in the south of Switzerland near the Italian border. We had hoped to find somewhere reasonably priced to spend the night, but we could find nothing suitable. In the end, late at night, we caught a train bound for northern Switzerland. We hoped we would be able to sleep on the train.
82 The porter was friendly and showed us to an empty compart-

ment. He explained that the window was broken and couldn't be shut, but that we could lie down and sleep. We thanked him and stretched out, one on each bench seat. Even at this late hour it was so hot that having the window open was a great relief.

We were very tired, fell asleep immediately, and slept soundly. Early the next morning we both woke up absolutely frozen through and completely stiff. We just couldn't understand how we could have become so cold during a warm summer night down there in southern Europe. Admittedly we only had thin summer clothes on, but still. . . . Gradually, as we sat there and shivered, despite the fact that it was not cold outside and that we had put on all the extra clothes we had, we realized what had happened. While we had been sleeping the train had crossed the Alps at the Saint Gotthard Pass, which lies at a height of 2,108 metres above sea level. With the window wide open the cold had really got through to us. We just couldn't fall asleep again — we were far too cold.

Even though we alighted from the train into the warm morning sun and had a cup of hot chocolate and went for a brisk walk, it took several hours before we felt warmed through.

Life is like that sometimes. It brings us sudden, unexpected, and occasionally drastic changes in circumstance. In such situations it is good to know that God's promises never fail, promises like the one in today's text.

PRAYER: Thank you, Lord, that you never leave us, however much may change around us.

'ASK FOR HELEN!'

Lead me, O Lord, in your righteousness.
PSALM 5:8

For many years June had the habit of praying in the morning after she had read her Bible. She had prayed the same sentence every morning, and meant it seriously every time she said it. She would pray: 'Lord, lead me today so that I can be of help to someone.' She noticed that when she said this in her prayer she experienced many wonderful things as she 'worked together with God', as she called it, in an effort to help others.

Even when she was on holiday she would pray this prayer. On one occasion she planned to spend a couple of weeks at a health centre. She had been there several times before and it was nice to meet again so many people she already knew among the staff. She hadn't been at the centre very long before she remembered Helen. Helen had helped out when June was there last, and they had talked together several times. She kept a look-out for Helen but she didn't seem to be there anymore. When June tried to put the thought of Helen out of her mind she seemed to hear a voice inside her saying, 'Ask for Helen.'

June did ask, but nobody seemed to know exactly where Helen lived now. Some thought she might be sick, others thought they had heard she lived in a house further away. June set off: she was not going to give up now. She had to ask her way several times before she met someone who thought they knew that Helen lived further down the road.

June tried the house, and the door was opened by a pale and sad Helen who at once recognized the friendly June. She invited her in and when they had hugged each other Helen burst into tears and said, 'I have lost my faith in God and I am so depressed I just don't want to live any more.' Now June understood why God had made her look for Helen. She sat down and began to explain what God had done for her and what God was like. Helen listened, and the more she listened to June — who knew God so personally — the more she began to realize that God was still there and that he cared about her and her problems. Before June left the house the two women prayed together and Helen felt she could face the future with new courage and a revived faith in Christ.

PRAYER: Lord, if there is someone I can help today, show me how to find that person and give me the right words to say.

BORING? THAT DEPENDS ON YOU!

I love the house where you live, O Lord, the place where your glory dwells.
PSALM 26:8

Twelve-year-old Marcus didn't think that church was a pleasant place. It was really hard to sit still during the service. He felt it was unkind of his parents to insist that he went every week. In the end he couldn't take any more. He was so angry when he arrived home after an unusually long service! His parents found the whole situation rather embarrassing as they had guests to dinner. Elderly people who probably wouldn't understand how a young boy felt.

One of the guests, however, smiled at Marcus and said that she could help him solve his problem once the meal was over. Marcus looked at the grey-haired lady and wondered what she would come up with. The two of them went out into the garden after dinner and Marcus decided to be polite and listen. The lady maintained that Marcus could do something to make the church service more interesting if he really wanted to. It depended more on Marcus than on the pastor, she said. He stared at her as she began to explain:

'You ought to take some paper and a pencil next week,' she said, 'and make a list of all the parts of the service you can take part in. You can take part in the singing, in giving an offering, by kneeling and praying to God.

'During the sermon there is much you can do to take part in that too.' Marcus looked surprised. The other advice had sounded rather obvious, but now he couldn't see what she was getting at. She smiled: 'I can give you a few hints. But you will think up many more on your own, once you have practised a bit.' Marcus was still wondering how he could take part in something as difficult as a sermon, but he didn't mind hearing suggestions.

'You can, for example, write down all the Bible texts the pastor mentions, or look them up and see how quickly you can find them and read them yourself. Or you can write a few words which will remind you of the stories or illustrations the pastor used in his sermon. You can write down all the words you don't understand and then look them up when you get home or ask your parents about them. Or you can write down the text you liked best and write it on a card in the afternoon, a card you drew yourself, and then send it to someone who is old or sick and couldn't come to church.'

PRAYER: Help me to feel that you are there in the church, Lord, when we worship you. Help me to get a blessing from the service and then pass it on.

HELPED OUT OF PRISON

But during the night an angel of the Lord opened the doors of the jail and brought them out. "Go, stand in the temple courts," he said, "and tell the people the full message of this new life."
ACTS 5:19, 20

God has, through the years, shown himself willing to help those who serve him. When such people have been prevented from carrying out the work God has sent them to do he has sometimes chosen to intervene. In the Bible you can read about several occasions when God helped his servants out of prison, sometimes by using angels. Even in modern times God has done similar things. Sometimes he uses people, sometimes angels.

Adoniram Judson pulled himself up off the prison floor where he had been kicked by the prison warden. He shook the dirt from his clothes and sat down to think over his strange situation. He was an American, a missionary on his way to India and Burma.

He had embarked in America bound for England on an English vessel which had been captured by the French who were at war with England. All those aboard the captured vessel were thrown into prison as prisoners of war. There they would have to sit and wait till the war was over — several years perhaps. But Judson was in a hurry. He wanted to get to his mission field and start preaching. While he was being led to the prison through the narrow streets of the little French town of Bayonne, Judson had continuously shouted out that he was not English and that he wanted to speak to the governor. He had a right to his freedom as America was not in the war. But no one heard him. The people by the roadside kicked him and spat at him. And now he sat there, helpless and with no rights.

In his mind's eye he could see the people of India waiting for him. He cried out to God: 'Dear Lord, get me out of this mess. It is your work I want to do. Help me to be able to do it.' Someone touched him on the shoulder. Judson spun round and found himself looking at a kind smiling face. It was no one he knew, but he understood that this was a friend. He had heard no sound or movement, so asked, 'How did you get in here? Who are you?' The only answer he received was the stranger throwing his cloak over Judson's shoulders and whispering the order, 'Run! There is an American ship in the harbour. Board her and you are safe.'

Judson didn't delay. He ran through the open cell door, down the empty prison corridor, out to the harbour and on to that American ship.

He never found out who it was that God had sent to save him. God had perhaps spoken to someone who had seen and understood what had happened when Judson had been calling out as he stumbled along the streets to the prison. He was very thankful to that brave man who had taken pity on him.

PRAYER: Thank you, God, that you are both willing and able to help us when we are in need.

THE TIDE

**He reached down from on high and took hold of me;
he drew me out of deep waters.**
PSALM 18:16

My father was floating on his back in the water, enjoying every minute of it. The sun shone from a clear blue sky. Sea-gulls glided effortlessly over the water. They looked so white against the blue sky. How wonderful to lie like this and go up and down on the gentle waves, relaxing and day-dreaming.

After some time he looked around to see where he was. He

found that he had floated uncomfortably far away from the beach. There was no one else swimming this far out. He began to swim with strong strokes towards the shore. But however hard he tried to swim, however much effort he put behind each stroke, he made no visible progress. He just wasn't getting anywhere. It seemed rather that the shoreline was getting further and further away instead of nearer. He soon realized why. The tide was going out fast and its pull was very strong. He knew now that he would really need to struggle to make it to safety, and set off once again with grim determination. My father was a good swimmer, but not used to doing long distances, so he soon began to feel more and more tired, and the shore was just as far away as before. No one had noticed his predicament. There was only one person who knew that he needed help and that was God. Father started to pray, 'Lord, give me the strength I need to swim back to the shore.'

He had rested on his back while he was talking to God. He turned to continue to swim and do battle with the tide. At first he thought he was seeing things. To his great surprise he now lay in the water almost next to the shore, in quite a different place from where he had been when he started to pray. He put his feet down to see if he could reach the bottom — he could! Slowly he made his way up onto the sands. How this had happened so fast he couldn't even explain to himself. He lay down on the beach to rest his weary body. After the struggle and tension he felt totally exhausted, but immensely thankful for the inexplicable way he had reached safety.

PRAYER: Thank you, Lord, for having power over the waters of the sea, and that you are ready when we cry to you for help.

UP IN THE MOUNTAINS

I sought the Lord, and he answered me; he delivered me from all my fears.
PSALM 34:4

Some summers ago we went on holiday in the mountains of Lapland, on the border between Sweden and Norway. We travelled with relatives and friends in three cars. Our little group included seven children, and they took turns travelling in the different cars to make the long trip less boring. We had all taken a long stop at Tärnaby, the mountain village in which the slalom skier Ingemar Stenmark grew up, and had made plans to drive a longer stretch along winding mountain roads and over into Norway. The trip would take about four hours.

We set off in convoy and hadn't travelled for more than about twenty minutes when something happened that I have never experienced before or since. It was as if someone had taken hold of me with firm, strong hands pressed around my heart. At the same time a voice inside me said, 'Kelvin isn't with you.' Kelvin, our eldest son, was then ten years old. I told my husband about this strong premonition. We were the last of the three cars, and so he speeded up to look into the other cars ahead to see if Kelvin was there. It was impossible to see who was who — all we could see in the back seats were the arms and legs of children having a lively time.

But I was convinced that God had been trying to tell me something very important, so when we got a chance to pass the other two cars on the narrow winding mountain road we made them both stop. Kelvin *wasn't* there — we had all thought he was in someone else's car and therefore had not checked as we drove off from Tärnaby.

We set off back to Tärnaby as fast as possible but the return journey seemed as though it took hours. At last the small village came into view. There was Kelvin, standing by the roadside, tear-stained and frightened. Two ladies were with him. It transpired that after Kelvin and the ladies had waited and worried for some time, they had decided to pray that God would send us back. And that is exactly what he had done. If God hadn't answered their prayers so markedly we would not have noticed that Kelvin was missing until we arrived in Norway four hours later.

PRAYER: Thank you, Lord, for hearing us when we pray and for helping us when we are in need.

A SELFLESS PRISONER

"Greater love has no-one than this, that one lay down his life for his friends."
JOHN 15:13

A hush had fallen over the prisoner-of-war camp. It had just been announced that someone had succeeded in escaping during the night. Everyone in the camp knew what that meant. There was a law there that every time someone escaped the prison warders had the right to kill ten prisoners. A grim way of retaliating since those punished were the innocent. The victims were chosen at random. Everyone sat in silence, wondering if it would be his turn this time.

The majority of the prisoners in this Polish camp were not there because of any crimes they had committed. This incident took place during the Second World War, when people were incarcerated merely because they were Jews, or had opinions Hitler did not agree with. These prisoners were ordinary people, innocent victims of hunger and torture in inhumane camps. Some found the whole situation so degrading and humiliating that they became discouraged to the extent of wanting to give up altogether. Some came to the point where they wanted to take their own lives rather than sit and wait for the next round of ill-treatment. However, they found that there were fellow prisoners who had enough inner strength to care about the fate of others and who tried to instil hope in the hopeless. One such caring prisoner was the Polish priest Maximilian Kolbe. His prisoner's number was 11670. To the Gestapo he was nothing more than a number, a number among thousands of others. The Gestapo had deprived him of his liberty, but they had not been able to take from him his love for his fellow men and his faith in God. He used all his available time in that terrible place to encourage and comfort the other prisoners, doing all he could to make life a little more bearable for them.

It was July 1941. Everyone was sitting, waiting, wondering which ten would be executed. An officer appeared with a list of ten names. One man on the list was Frank Gajoconiczek. When he heard his name read out he began to weep quietly. He would never see his wife and family again. He had been hoping so much, dreaming every day about his family reunion. Now all his dreams were destroyed in an instant. Kolbe tried to comfort him. Then the priest had an idea — a wonderful and selfless idea. He would be the tenth man instead of Frank. The prison warder accepted the plan and Kolbe was executed to save the life of a fellow human being.

PRAYER: Thank you, Lord, for dying on my behalf so that I can be saved and have eternal life. Help me to understand more of what it cost for you to do this. Help me to value your sacrifice more highly.

SECRETS

"But when you give to the needy, do not let your left hand know what your right hand is doing, so that your giving may be in secret. Then your Father, who sees what is done in secret, will reward you."
MATTHEW 6:3, 4

One of the most exciting things in life is to do something for someone else in secret. Marion discovered this when she was 13 years old. Up to then she had often thought life was dull, to say the least. Every day was just like every other day — boring and meaningless. She lived in the country where there was not much in the way of excitement, and not many young people of her own age.

Then, almost by chance, she had the idea of a new exciting 'hobby'. She soon developed it into a well-organized programme of action which she called her secret with God. The fact that it was only her and God who knew about it made it even more exciting. Marion put a lot of time into what she called her reconnaissance work. She tried to find out who in her village was sick, who was sad, which home had lost someone close to them, or where there was a mother who was tired and overworked looking after small children. Once she had found a 'project' she set about planning how she could do something to help — without anyone finding out that it was her who had done it.

It took her some further work to find out which time of the day or night she could go into action without being noticed. Sometimes she had to wait until it was dark, while other times she could work during the day. She would perhaps place a bunch of flowers she had picked from her garden on the doorstep of someone who was depressed, and tied to it would be a relevant Bible text. Sometimes she took in the washing for someone when it started to rain and no one was at home. She might bake something special and put it on the doorstep of a stressed mother so that she would have something nourishing to give her family without having to do extra work.

Sometimes Marion would hide nearby and keep a look out to see how the people reacted when they discovered what had been done for them. The joy she felt when she saw the surprise and appreciation on the faces of those she had tried to help cannot be described. You have to experience it for yourself in order to understand. Try it and see!

PRAYER: Lord, make me more aware of the needs of those around me today.

ON THE TRAIN

Preach the Word; be prepared in season and out of season; correct, rebuke and encourage — with great patience and careful instruction.
2 TIMOTHY 4:2

Every time I go on long train journeys I wonder if I will meet someone I can help or whom I can tell about Jesus.

Once when I was about to set out on a five-hour trip in the evening I was so tired that I decided to sit in a corner and not speak to anyone. I had given a three-hour lecture on how to interest children in the Bible, and felt completely drained. I decided that if I did have to talk to someone I would not talk about religious things. I couldn't find a corner seat, however, and had to sit by the aisle. Just across from me sat a young Canadian tourist who wanted advice about where to get off and what to see. The guard was not very helpful so I thought I would fill him in on some details. When I had finished I tried to settle down comfortably to doze a bit.

Before I could get that far the young Canadian spoke to me again. He seemed to want someone to talk to. It wasn't long before he started to get onto religious subjects and my first thought was: Why tonight when I'm so tired? He told me how he had been converted and what had made him start to live a Christian life. He went on to say how much Jesus meant to him personally in his everyday life, and how God had answered one of his prayers as recently as the day before. I sat back and listened, marvelling at his simple and natural way of talking to others about his friend Jesus. It also made me feel ashamed that I had even thought of not wanting to witness just because I felt tired.

We had a long talk as we travelled and exchanged addresses. A few weeks later I received a letter from him in which he described his holiday in Amsterdam. What do you think he wrote about? All the tourist sights he had seen? No. He explained that he had met a despairing young man who wanted to take his own life. He had spent three whole days talking to this Dutch youth about God and the help he can give us, and the depressed young man had found new hope and courage.

This made me think whether I allow my holidays, my meeting with people, to be a continuous witness for Christ as this young man did.

PRAYER: Lord, help me to take every opportunity to witness about you and to help my fellow men, even when I don't feel like it — and even when I'm on holiday!

BEHIND THE SCENES

"My peace I give you. . . . Do not let your hearts be troubled and do not be afraid."
JOHN 14:27

When we want to invite a friend or relative to come and stay with us we can phone or write to them. If they decide they would like to come they simply get in the car, or take the bus or train. It's that easy in our part of the world.

If, however, in the past you had wanted to invite someone from one of the Eastern bloc countries things immediately become much more complicated. I am good friends with a Polish university lecturer and his wife. I had been over to visit them and wanted to invite them to come and stay with our family. In order for my Polish friends to apply for a passport and permission to take a holiday outside Poland, I had to produce different documents with official and very expensive stamps, with signatures from   91 various authorities, both Polish and our own. All this took a long time. To this add the four weeks it took the post to reach the correct addresses in Poland during the state of emergency in 1982.

My Polish friends were among many who didn't have the luxury of a telephone. All they could do was wait and wait for the right letters to come, and with them the valuable documents they needed. While they waited they worried and wondered. Was I doing anything? Was I really interested in helping them arrange this very special holiday abroad? Why hadn't I already sent the papers they so badly needed? For two long months they had to wait. Then they received the proof that I had been doing all I could to arrange things for them.

Sometimes we become impatient with God. We ask him for help or advice and just because we do not receive an answer immediately we think he hasn't heard us or that he no longer cares. Sometimes it can take a long time before we see clearly how God has been working on our behalf, behind the scenes, though we were totally unaware of it at the time.

PRAYER: Lord, give us more patience and trust in you.

PENICILLIN

O Lord Almighty, blessed is the man who trusts in you.
PSALM 84:12

Dr. Kazen works at a leprosy hospital in Sierra Leone, West Africa. He is a Christian doctor who has specialized in treating people with this disease. Sometimes people who have contracted leprosy only need short periods of treatment with medications. But occasionally they have to spend several years at the hospital. This is particularly so in cases where hands and feet have become completely ruined by the disease. In such cases Dr. Kazen performs operations to try to restore at least some use to these spoiled hands. It's a difficult job but very rewarding.

In order to treat the disease special medicine is needed, medicine which is not made in Africa and has to be ordered from abroad. On one occasion Dr. Kazen had ordered a special penicillin which he used. When the long-awaited medicines arrived at last he eagerly opened the large consignment, but to his great disappointment he had been sent the wrong kind of penicillin. He now had on his hands a large amount of medicine he couldn't use.

He didn't want to throw the medicine away but wondered what he could do with it. He kept wondering why he had been sent the wrong kind, and began to pray about the matter. Soon he felt impressed to drive all that penicillin to another Christian hospital.

They had all types of patients and were more like a general hospital. Perhaps they could use the consignment. He loaded everything into the car and drove the long distance to the hospital. When he finally arrived he sought out the director and told him about the medicine he had received and for which he had no use. The director looked at Dr. Kazen in amazement, and asked him to repeat what type of medicine it was and its strength. When Dr. Kazen repeated these facts the man's face showed both astonishment and joy. He explained that the whole staff of the hospital had gathered in prayer just a few days earlier. They were in great need of exactly this type and strength of penicillin and had asked God to help them get it quickly. Now God had answered their prayer. It was hard to know who was happiest — Dr. Kazen, who had been able to be a part of an answer to prayer, or the board of the hospital who felt strongly that God had both heard and answered them in their need.

PRAYER: Lord, we praise your name that you hear us when we pray.

OUTSIDE WOOLWORTHS
I love the Lord, for he heard my voice; he heard my cry.
PSALM 116:1

Martha had agreed with her 20-year-old son that they would meet outside the main entrance to Woolworths. It was an easy place to get to and therefore a good rendezvous. They had decided to meet at four o'clock in order to get home in time for supper. They had quite a long drive home and Martha was anxious to get back early because she had to go to a meeting as soon as tea was over.

When Martha had finished her shopping she went and stood outside the main entrance to the large Woolworths store. She had arrived rather early but that didn't matter, her son Kenneth would soon be there. However, time passed and he didn't appear. She reasoned that he must have been delayed somewhere and just hoped he wouldn't be too long. She was in a hurry. He didn't appear. Martha then remembered that there was another smaller entrance on a side street and she ran round to see if he had misunderstood her and was waiting by that door instead. But he wasn't there either. She rushed back to the main entrance in case he had turned up while she was gone. He hadn't. The problem was that Kenneth was slightly mentally handicapped and sometimes misremembered instructions. If he lost his bearings in town he might also find it hard to home in on the right place. In the main he was surprisingly good at managing on his own, but his mother didn't want him wandering around lost, looking for her. She returned to the side entrance. Still no Kenneth. Now it was getting late. Martha 93 didn't have time to wait any longer, but she couldn't leave her son there without help either.

So she turned to God in her dilemma. 'Help me to find Kenneth soon', she prayed simply and waited for God to tell her what to do. She was impressed to start walking in the opposite direction to the way she had already taken. She crossed the road by a set of traffic lights. Just as she stepped onto the pavement on the other side of the road she saw Kenneth cross a street further down and disappear. A few seconds earlier or later and she wouldn't have seen him. Now she hurried along and soon caught up with him. He had been waiting for her since four o'clock at another entrance to Woolworths which she hadn't considered as it was the goods entrance! How long it would have taken to find him in this large town once he had set off on his own no one knows. With God's timely help Martha didn't need to find out. Talk about split-second timing!

PRAYER: Lord, sometimes we are like lost children. Your guidance day by day means so much to us. Thank you for your faithfulness.

A LARGE HAND

"The Lord's right hand has done mighty things!" I will not die but live, and will proclaim what the Lord has done.
PSALM 118:16, 17

Some people seem to be more prone to ending up in dangerous situations than others. Pastor Rudge was just such a person. His life was filled with exciting experiences. He was Australian and had started to work among the people who lived on the small islands off the coast of Australia. To do the job he had a large motor boat which was seaworthy even in rough seas. The boat could seat eight to ten people.

One day when he was going to one of the more distant islands he had eight people with him. As the trip was a long one, the man in charge of the boat had brought extra fuel which he kept in a large petrol can in the middle of the boat. When they had covered quite a distance and all they could see around them was still the open sea, the motor stopped — the fuel in the tank was used up. The man took the petrol can and started to pour fuel into the tank so that they could continue their journey. Forgetting that the engine would be very hot, he just poured the fuel straight in. There was an enormous explosion and within seconds the whole back of the boat was in flames.

The passengers were blown forward by the explosion. Confused but unharmed they huddled together as tightly as they could in the front of the boat, wondering how long it would take for it to sink. They wondered if it was possible to swim to the nearest island — but it wasn't even in sight! There was a lot to think about as they held on to each other so as not to fall into the sea. Even for those who could swim, these waters were far from being a friendly bathing place. There were sharks that took an active interest in humans given the chance. There was no other boat in sight.

The boat could only last a few more minutes. They needed help at once if they were to survive. All eyes turned heavenward as Pastor Rudge began to pray. God was their only hope and they knew it. They all cried out to him. Would he intervene? If so, how? Would someone come and save them? They held their breath in tense expectation when they had finished praying.

They turned their eyes to the fire which was making its way towards them.

Suddenly they all saw it.

No one could actually describe it properly, but it looked like a large hand which was lowered over the flames, choking the fire. In a few seconds the fire was out. It all happened so quickly they could hardly believe it. Had God laid his mighty hand over their little boat to save them from certain death?

PRAYER: Thank you, God, for caring about us even when we make mistakes and put ourselves in danger.

MASTER CRAFTSMAN

And the Lord God formed man from the dust of the ground and breathed into his nostrils the breath of life, and man became a living being.
GENESIS 2:7

The piece of marble stood there, large and beautiful, but seemingly completely ruined. The sculptor had measured incorrectly when he was starting to work on the stone and had made a large triangular hole near the base of the block of marble. What could it be used for now, with a big hole like that at its base? The stone had been so expensive; what an awful waste. This was the situation in Florence, Italy, in 1501.

At that time there was another young sculptor who had begun to make a name for himself in Rome. Now he was called to Florence to save the situation. The young man was taken to look at the stone. He stood before the large block which had been there for decades. Would he be able to make something out of it, or was it spoilt for ever? He spent many hours in front of the stone as he thought and calculated. One day he decided what he would do. He had wooden walls erected round the stone so that he could work without people standing and staring. Day after day he worked away with his tools. His hammer blows could be heard as they hit the chisel, and bits of marble flew in all directions, crashing against the wooden screen. At first people were curious, but as time passed they got used to the work going on behind the screen.

The day came when he had finished, and those who had ordered the work came to look at it. There stood a beautiful statue of David in his youth, a David who stands looking at Goliath. That far-too-tall stone was just the right height for the slim, tall, athletic David. He looked almost alive, so well formed was he. All his muscles were tensed, ready for action. What about that big hole? It had become the gap between David's muscular, vigorous legs. A master craftsman had transformed a total failure into a masterpiece which was proudly set in front of the Palazzo Vecchio in Florence. The master's name? Michelangelo, the almost self-taught young sculptor who, with this and other masterpieces, became world famous.

We all admire people who can transform stone into something which looks alive, but God made man out of the dust of the ground. And he didn't just make him *look* alive, but become actual living flesh.

PRAYER: Thank you, our Master Craftsman, for your touch which has made us and given us life.

DANGEROUS WAVES

I will instruct you and teach you in the way you should go; I will counsel you and watch over you.
PSALM 32:8

How wonderful it was to rush forward over the warm water on a small surfboard; even if it felt as though all the skin was being rubbed off your knees every time a wave threw you up on the sandy beach! I had borrowed a surf-board and after many mistakes had finally learnt to jump on it at just the right moment and lie down with my stomach on the surf-board and let the wave carry me back to the beach. There on the palm-lined beach outside Accra, the capital of Ghana, you could surf just like they do in films. It was very exciting.

But it was not all fun. You could always see three surf waves at a time. When you stood inside the first one the water came up to your knees, and already at that point there was a frighteningly strong suction in the water, not pulling you towards the shore in the direction of the waves, but out to sea, a kind of undercurrent. In order to surf you jumped onto the second wave, and then the water was almost up to your hips. Any deeper than that and you just couldn't stand — the outward pull was so strong.

A few days before I arrived there, four crew members from a British airline company had swum past the third wave in order to get to calmer water. They were never seen again.

Because the waters are so dangerous there is always a man on watch to keep an eye on the swimmers. He has a loud whistle which he blows to warn anyone who starts to go too far out. If you value your life you obey his warning and keep in safe waters.

PRAYER: Lord, you also try to warn me about dangers and lead me safely. Help me to heed your warnings and stay close by your side.

THE LARGE ANGEL

The angel of the Lord encamps around those who fear him, and he delivers them.
PSALM 34:7

At the turn of the century a young couple moved to Sweden. The pretty young wife was Italian and her husband was French. They both had dark eyes and dark hair. It was very evident that they were not Swedes. They settled in a country area on the east coast where the husband started work at a blacksmiths. They tried to learn Swedish and make friends with their neighbours, but it wasn't easy. They felt like strangers, outcasts.

Then one day there was a row between the workers at the blacksmiths. No one knows what actually brought it on, but the result was that everyone in the village was angry with the Frenchman, very angry indeed. That evening the village men decided to give the intruder the once-over. They wanted rid of him. They had drunk quite a lot of alcohol before they set off to the little crofter's holding where the young foreign couple lived. The couple could hear the angry men approaching and realized the danger they were in. The mob outside began to call to the Frenchman to come out or they would destroy the house. His wife pleaded with him to stay indoors. The men out there were so angry she was afraid they would kill her husband. In the end he went out to meet them so that they wouldn't break their way in.

The young wife was so frightened that she threw herself down on her knees and began to pray for help. They had no one else who could come to their aid. She was a devout Christian and now, when she began to pray, a great calm came over her. She felt sure God would help them. While she was praying the room grew lighter and brighter. She opened her eyes to see what could be causing this strong light. No wonder she had felt such peace in her heart while the men outside were yelling at her husband! There in her little living room stood an angel. She couldn't really see him properly because he was so bright. The young woman 97 particularly noticed how large the angel was. It was as if his being and the light he radiated filled the whole room. Her tears of joy shone in the bright light. For a moment she had forgotten the danger outside. When she began to listen to what was going on she noticed that the drunk and angry men were now on their way back to the village. It wasn't long before everything was quiet again. But what had happened to her husband? She was no longer afraid, only curious to know what God had done. Then the door opened and he came back in, unharmed. In that same instant the angel disappeared, the beautiful angel who had given this lonely and frightened woman comfort and strength.

PRAYER: You have promised to protect us if we stay close to you, Lord. Thank you for your angels' presence, even if we do not always see them.

THE CARAVAN

I will lie down and sleep in peace, for you alone, O Lord, make me dwell in safety.
PSALM 4:8

The girls and I reluctantly left the camp fire and made our way back to our sleeping quarters. It had been a lovely finish to a day of fun at the scout camp set alongside a big lake in wooded landscape. It would be nice to crawl into bed in our tiny old caravan. As one of the three girls in my group was almost blind it was easier for her to manage in a caravan than in a tent like the other guides.

When we opened the door we were met by an awful smell, and wondered if someone had thrown in a stink bomb. The smell was so strong that it made us feel ill. It smelt a bit like gas, but we hadn't used the gas in the caravan for several days. Whatever it was, we couldn't sleep there. We called to the leader of the group who came over. He was a policeman and knew at once that it was gas that had leaked into the caravan.

We disconnected the gas system and aired the caravan thoroughly. Inside I felt thankfulness well up, thankfulness to God. What if the gas had started to leak while we were asleep? We would perhaps not have noticed it before it was too late. It just didn't bear thinking of what would have happened if one of the girls in my charge had been injured, or worse! How awful it would have been to have to phone home to the parents and say that something had gone wrong.

We live in a world which is full of dangers, some of which we are not even aware of. Every evening when we go to bed we ought to thank God for his protection during the day. And thank him for the protection he gives during the long night.

PRAYER: Thank you for your watchcare at all times, Lord. Thank you for the many times you have kept me from harm.

CLOSE EARLY TONIGHT

They were all trying to frighten us . . . . But I prayed, "Now strengthen my hands."
NEHEMIAH 6:9

It was Friday and the nurse at the mission clinic was working as usual, taking care of the long line of patients waiting for treatment. As the morning progressed the nurse felt more and more strongly that she should tidy up and clean the clinic earlier than usual. She had never done so before, but it was almost as if a voice was exhorting her to do it now. So she did as she felt compelled and got everything done by twelve. Her young Ethiopian helpers had no objection to going home early that day.

At 1.30 an army jeep drove up to the mission compound. Ethiopia was at war, and the fighting was not far away from the clinic. In fact in this sort of war it is hard to know where the two sides in the conflict were. The men in the jeep said that they were from the Ministry of Health and had been sent to check up on all the malpractices the clinic was guilty of. The Swedish nurse smiled warmly and invited them to come and look round. She knew she had nothing to be ashamed of. The men seemed a little irritated over the fact that everything was so neat and tidy. They then started to accuse her of using medicine which was past its shelf-life. She opened up all her medicine cupboards and asked them to check for themselves. In her heart she sent up a prayer of thanks to God that she had recently gone through everything and disposed of all medicines with expired dates. They found nothing amiss in her medicine cupboards. Then they began to accuse her of lying about the number of patients she was treating. They pointed out that it was impossible for her on her own to treat 2,000 patients during the month of May. The young nurse took out her case record book in which she noted down details of all the patients she treated every day, even though this was not required of such a small clinic. No doctor ever came there. The men read sullenly through her notes. It all seemed true enough.

Then came the next question: 'How many dressers do you have working for you?' 'None', she replied. The only helpers she had were young school leavers she had taught to help her in the running of the clinic. Now the men were really angry. They demanded to see her staff. The nurse had sent them home at twelve o'clock, and she honestly did not know where in the tiny outlying villages they all lived. All she could suggest was that if the men really needed to see them they must look for themselves. But the men drove off without bothering, seemingly too angry to care. Now that the war was at its height dressers were in great demand and they were forced to go to the war front. The jeep had hardly been gone an hour before the clinic helpers and their families came back to join the nurse in thankfulness to God for being left in peace.

PRAYER: Thank you, Lord, that though people try to spoil your work, you can protect and give wisdom and courage.

KEEP AWAY FROM TEMPTATION
Do not give the devil a foothold.
EPHESIANS 4:27

David had one weakness — sweets. He ate as many as he could get from his friends, his mother and what he could afford to buy himself. Sometimes none of his friends, nor his mother, had any sweets to offer him. It seemed as though these catastrophes coincided with David's lack of pocket money.

One such day, when he was feeling very sorry for himself, he thought he might feel a bit better and have less of a craving for sweets if he went into the shop and just looked at the sweets. It would be good to check what was on special offer, so that he knew what to buy next pocket-money day.

He stood there in front of the shelves laden with chocolates, toffees and jellies, and his mouth began to water. The longer he stood there the worse it became. In the end the temptation became too strong for him and when no one was watching he took a small bar of chocolate and left the shop with it in his pocket.

Now he had something sweet to eat, but inside he felt quite strange. For the first time in his life he had shoplifted. It hurt in his chest when he thought about it, and he didn't feel so keen on eating the chocolate. After a while he took a bite anyway. It didn't taste as good as usual. Strange. . . .

A week or so passed and David had nearly forgotten the whole episode. Then came one of those days when all his money was used up. He went and stood in front of the shelves of sweets again. He thought he wouldn't be tempted to take anything after having had such trouble with his conscience last time. But he hadn't stood there long before he could no longer resist taking a *larger* bar of chocolate. He avoided being seen this time too, and the bar of chocolate didn't taste as bad as the last one he had stolen. Perhaps he was becoming hardened, he thought, but the idea didn't make him glad.

Now David happily went into the shop every day. It was, after all, cheaper to steal than to buy, and it all seemed so easy. His conscience had stopped bothering him now. He had also become less careful. That's when he got caught. The owner of the shop spotted him and when he checked his pockets found that he had several kinds of sweets hidden there. David was so ashamed. How could he, who had grown up in a Christian home, become a shoplifter? The shop owner wrote down David's name and phone number. Then he gave him a piece of advice: 'Don't come in here if you haven't the money for what you want. Why stand there and let yourself be tempted?'

PRAYER: Give me the strength to keep away from that which tempts me to sin.

A HELPING HAND

"Call upon me in the day of trouble; I will deliver you."
PSALM 50:15

Why had I been silly enough to get into this situation? I couldn't keep afloat any longer, I was exhausted. The more I thought about it the more frightened I became, and the harder it was to swim properly. I tried to grab hold of the edge of the large swimming pool, but every time I had almost reached it the next big wave came and pulled me away and down once again.

As a teenager on holiday with friends in Switzerland, I had decided to spend the afternoon at a large outdoor swimming pool. I had gone there alone and thought it was nice to be free to do what I wanted, when I wanted. I had swum a long time and had stretched out on the grass completely exhausted. Then the loudspeakers announced that the wave-machine was to be turned on. I had never been in a pool with artificial waves, so I jumped into the water again. But I had never imagined the waves would be so high and so powerful. I was far too tired to keep my head above water, and too scared to relax and float. I had thought it was fun to be there all alone, but now I longed for someone to notice that I needed help. Someone keeping an eye on me, who could pull me up onto the side.

The water washed over my head once more and my nose and mouth filled with chlorinated water. I was near the edge of the pool but simply couldn't get a grip on anything. The edge was too high and the waves too strong.

My head came up out of the water again. I saw a hand stretched down right in front of me. Then a man's voice said in English, 'Do you want a hand up?' I managed a weak 'Yes'. The next moment I lay on the ground next to the pool, trying to get my breath back. Then I thought I must thank the man for helping me. I looked around to see where he was. There was no one standing round the pool, only people sunning themselves on the grass further away.

I still don't know who the man was. Nor have I stopped wondering how he happened to speak English right in the middle of Switzerland. All I know for sure is that God sent him to me when I needed help most.

PRAYER: Thank you, Lord, for all the times you have intervened and helped us in dangerous situations. Thank you that we can know, even today, that you are with us.

BOASTING

May I never boast except in the cross of our Lord Jesus Christ.
GALATIANS 6:14

'My dad's car can go faster than your dad's car.' 'My dad is stronger than your dad.' I'm sure you've heard small children boast like this. They so badly want to have something better than the others. When we get a little older we boast in a different way. We try to make others think that we are best at a certain subject in school. We have the latest hair style, or the most modern ten-gear bike, or we have the biggest home computer which has more and better programmes than any of our classmates.

It seems to be a human weakness to try to be better than others in some area or other. There are some people who put a lot of time and money into beating world records to get a mention in the *Guiness Book of Records*. There you can read about people who have run farther than several marathons put together. One person has swum 3,000km down the Mississippi river. Others have danced for over twenty-four weeks, carried bricks, paddled in a bathtub, flown large kites, pushed prams many kilometres. . . . The list is almost endless. You can try to be best in practically any area. You can even be the best in the village at rolling eggs unbroken down a hill!

The strange thing about boasting is that while people like to boast themselves, everyone dislikes it intensely in others. When someone starts to boast we immediately think he or she is trying to make themself seem important, and if someone boasts too much we end up avoiding them.

Paul was a highly educated man and a very energetic apostle and missionary. He had been through all sorts of exciting and dangerous experiences in his work for the Lord. When you think of all his exploits in the cause of God's work, he had a lot to boast about. But he *didn't* boast. He wrote today's text where he explains what he feels is the only thing worth boasting about. Do you agree with him?

PRAYER: Lord, make me more humble when I speak. Make me more keen to talk about what you have done, and not about myself.

QUEEN VICTORIA

All our righteous acts are like filthy rags.
ISAIAH 64:6

The story is told of Queen Victoria, who reigned from 1837 to 1901, and her visit to a paper mill. She was interested to see in detail how the different types of paper were made. The manager showed her round the whole mill. She followed the process from beginning to end, from the pulp being boiled and dissolved, till it was rolled out in the form of thin dry paper.

During the walk round the mill the Queen and her guide happened to pass a store-room, the door to which was slightly ajar. Queen Victoria stopped and looked in, surprised to see the piles of dirty old rags stacked there. She asked the manager why he had such dirty rags on the premises. He explained briefly that they were part of the raw material for making paper.

Some days after this visit to the paper mill, Queen Victoria received a small parcel. She opened the envelope which accompanied it and the letter said simply: 'This is paper made from the rags Your Majesty saw in the store-room.' The Queen wondered what the paper would look like and opened the parcel with interest. There lay the whitest, thinnest and loveliest writing paper she had ever seen. What a transformation! It was quite incredible.

It is an even greater wonder that God can transform our sinful lives into something holy and pure. But God can only cleanse and forgive us when we ask him to do so. The rags had no choice, but you do, and you must do the choosing.

PRAYER: Make me willing, Lord to be cleansed by you. Forgive me for everything I have done which has dirtied my life. Make me clean and holy.

WHAT WERE THEY LOOKING FOR?

"For the eyes of the Lord range throughout the earth to strengthen those whose hearts are fully committed to him."
2 CHRONICLES 16:9

My train was soon to pass the border between two Eastern European countries. First came several passport controls carried out by officials working in groups. They took time to read through all the pages in each passport. To my surprise the officials had my name written down on a list they carried with them. I was obviously expected!

After some delays several customs officials boarded the train. Having travelled quite a bit in the West I know what customs people usually look for — cigarettes, alcohol and other things that have to have duty paid on them. But these officials had completely different things on their minds. When they came to the compartment where I sat with seven younger girls whose language I could not speak, everything became absolutely quiet. It was as though the girls hardly dared to breathe. The customs officials looked thoughtfully at the bulging baggage up on the racks. They asked a few questions about some of the larger bags, and the biggest one had to be lifted down and opened so that they could look into it. Next one of the officials took a stick with a sharp blade at one end and poked it between the bags on the rack. Then a sharp command was given and all the girls got up from their seats, and so did I. The officials lifted each seat to see if there was anything under them. I wonder if you have guessed what they were looking for.

Gradually the train arrived at the border station where it stood and waited for almost an hour. I noticed that there was a lot of activity outside the train, so I opened a window and leant out to see what was going on. Then I got a chance to see something I had previously only read about in books. Military police were moving about with strong torches and metal poles, checking the whole of the long train's undercarriage, particularly the big hubs over the wheels. Have you guessed yet what they were looking for? People! People who might be trying to cross the border in order to make their way to a free country.

Today's text says that God also looks for people, but for completely different reasons. Read the text again. What a difference!

PRAYER: Thank you, God, for keeping an eye on me and for supplying the strength I need.

AN UNUSUAL WAY OF WITNESSING

"Give to the one who asks you, and do not turn away from the one who wants to borrow from you."
MATTHEW 5:42

In the village there was only one person who claimed to be a Christian. Everyone thought he was a strange old man. He hadn't had many years schooling and sometimes he found it difficult to explain different things in the Bible to the villagers when they purposely put tricky questions to him. He often became confused, but they noticed that he was never angry with them, however much they teased him. They reasoned that that was obviously because he was a bit strange.

The old man wanted to witness for his faith but he didn't know how to set about it with these villagers who always managed to confuse him. He obviously wasn't too good at explaining or teaching. The only thing he could do, he decided in the end, was to *live* like a Christian in the hope that that would be of help to someone.

It was quite a distance from the small village to the nearest shop in the town, so now and then it was necessary to borrow things like sugar or flour from a neighbour until the next visit to town. People borrowed from the old man. After some time the neighbours began to talk about him, saying how stupid he must be. He completely forgot what he had lent people and never asked for anything back. How forgetful!

More and more of the villagers noticed this and some began to take advantage of his kindness and borrowed all sorts of things, including tools which were expensive for a man on his low income. Others borrowed to see how much they could get away with before he realized what was going on.

The old man understood everything but said nothing. He just smiled kindly and kept on lending. In the end they became curious. He didn't seem to be stupid, so why did he go along with all this?

One day one of his neighbours asked him outright. He replied by quoting today's text. Soon everyone in the village had discussed his strange attitude. They began to get a new kind of respect for the old man. Some even began to ask him questions about the Bible, serious questions, and he answered as best he could. Now no one laughed at him. They began to listen instead.

PRAYER: Lord, help me to show people that I belong to you just by the way I live and treat others.

DANGER

Keep me safe, O God, for in you I take refuge.
PSALM 16:1

When you live in the rain forest areas of West Africa you are always aware of the different dangers lurking around. You always have to be on the look-out not to tread on something like a scorpion, or put your hand into something lying where you cannot see properly. It soon becomes a habit to check your bed before you get into it to see that there are no dangerous occupants! Even though you don't go around feeling frightened, you are very much aware that you need God's protection.

At the school the houses where the teachers lived had mosquito netting on the window to keep out insects which carry tropical diseases. My bedroom window had netting but there were several holes in it. It doesn't matter very much, I thought. The climbing plants just outside the window, with their leaves and branches would almost cover the holes. I reasoned that creepy-crawlies would have a hard job finding their way through. As time passed I forgot the holes completely and became less careful about checking my bedroom before I got into bed and put out the paraffin lamp.

One day I had been visited by some children who had played around in my room and by the time they left it seemed as though everything was down on the floor. It looked like a disaster area. I decided to set about clearing up the mess at once. You could hardly walk on the floor, it was so cluttered with books and things. When I had picked up most of the stuff, my mind on other things, I noticed I had forgotten to pick up my long, thick tie-belt. The children must have played with this too, I thought, as I crossed the room to pick it up and put it away. As I bent down to take hold of it the long green 'belt' began to move just as my hand was about to touch it. It was not the belt but a two-metre-long, thin green tree viper, a very poisonous snake. It had obviously climbed up the creepers in the garden and found a hole in the netting and decided to come into the room. I was so frightened that all I could do was call for help. I didn't dare move in case the viper bit me on the leg. The garden boy was nearby and came to my aid brandishing his machete knife in one hand and a mop in the other. With the latter he distracted the snake so that he could kill it properly. He was used to this sort of thing and knew the tricks of the trade.

When I went to bed that night I carefully checked everywhere to make sure there were no more snakes. The next day someone came and mended the holes in my window netting. With thankfulness to God I thought about all the months the holes had

106

been there when snakes could have come in at night without me being able to see and avoid them.

PRAYER: Thank you, Lord, for all the times you have saved my life, even the occasions when I was unaware of any danger.

THE LITTLE ONES

"If anyone causes one of these little ones who believe in me to sin, it would be better for him to be thrown into the sea with a large millstone tied around his neck."
MARK 9:42

Thomas had a little echo. When he laughed at something, his echo laughed. When he asked his mother for a biscuit his echo did too. His echo was very sweet. She had a round face, large dark eyes and long curly hair. According to Thomas she was the world's nicest little sister. She wasn't more than 3 years old while Thomas was 12. Sometimes he got tired of her always wanting to do exactly what he did. When she was not allowed to accompany him somewhere or other she cried. On the whole he loved her very much and basked in the admiration she showed for him.

One day Thomas found a new friend, a boy his own age who had just moved in nearby. This boy was unlike Thomas in a number of ways. He swore quite a lot and was rude to his parents and his teachers. Thomas didn't like this side of his new friend, but otherwise they got on very well and had great fun together. After a short while Thomas's mother began to notice that he was changing. He answered her impatiently and harshly sometimes, things he had not done before. One day when he hit his head on a cupboard door he swore, to his own surprise and his mother's disappointment. Mother tried to talk to Thomas about the way he was changing, but he didn't want to listen. He simply didn't believe her, and didn't want to either. He began to stay away from home, and had less time for his little sister.

One day when he sat at the kitchen table having breakfast he heard something which made him almost choke over his food. His dear little sister was obviously worked up about something. But he must have heard wrong — such a nice little girl surely wouldn't use swear words and talk to her mother in such an unpleasant way? She had never been like this before! The more he listened to his little sister as she shouted in the hall, the more he thought the words and phrases sounded familiar. They were exactly the same as those used by his new friend, and as Thomas himself had obviously used more than he realized. Thomas was horrified. His mother had been right. He had changed, and on top of that he was spoiling another person who looked up to him 107 and whom he loved. Not till then did he realize what a great responsibility he had as the older brother.

PRAYER: May I be a good example to those who look to me for a lead. Help me not to lead others into bad habits.

GUARDS ON THE TRAIN

Remember those in prison as if you were their fellow prisoners, and those who are ill-treated as if you yourselves were suffering.
HEBREWS 13:3

Some years ago the train which was to take me to East Berlin had stood still for an unusually long time. The woman who shared the sleeping compartment with me was Romanian and could understand most of what the passengers out in the corridor were saying. Gradually, by piecing together a little information from here and there, we understood that our two carriages were to stand here and wait for another train which would come in about five hours. Till then it was a case of sitting and waiting. We could not ask questions either. The guard just refused to answer.

After a while I was so tired of just sitting that I decided to go out into the corridor to stretch my legs and take in a change of view. Then I saw something very strange. There, in the corridor, stood a military policeman armed with a gun. The gun was not slung back over his shoulder but held in his hands ready for firing. I tried to pretend he wasn't there but still thought it best not to do anything which could be misinterpreted by this alert young man. I stood for a while by the window and tried to find out where we were. There was no train staff to elicit any information from, so I tried to find things out myself. I saw that our two carriages stood right out in the countryside on a dead-end siding. Between the trees I could see a small village about 1km away. What surprised me most was that at the beginning and end of our short two-carriage train there stood two armed military police. They too held their guns ready. It was obviously not thought to be enough to have armed men in both carriages — we had to be guarded from the outside too. They were making sure no one could contact us during the six long hours that we had to stand and wait there.

An hour or so later I decided to go down to the toilet which was situated at one end of the carriage. When I arrived it was engaged so I stood and waited. I must have been gone too long. The military policeman with his lowered rifle came round the corner and angrily asked me what I was doing. It took some talking to persuade him I was only queuing. He remained standing there with his gun aimed at me, to make sure I was not going to do anything with which he didn't agree. It was quite a shattering experience to see with my own eyes the blatant lack of freedom which existed in those days in countries which are so close to ours.

PRAYER: Thank you, Father, that we are able to live in a free country. We pray today for those who are still oppressed, and particularly for Christians who are imprisoned for their faith.

A SONG IN THE NIGHT

By day the Lord directs his love, at night
his song is with me.
PSALM 42:8

Thomas lay on his bed, turning this way and that. He just could not go back to sleep. He put the light on to see what time it was. It was just 2am. He put out the light and tried to find a comfortable position so that he would fall asleep again. If only he could shut out the idea that kept cropping up in his mind. It was such a silly idea, more like a feeling than an idea actually, so it was best to try to think of something else. Easier said than done. Instead of getting weaker, the idea grew into a conviction. He sat up in bed just to make sure he was awake. He was, and the idea on his mind was going to give him no peace at all!

Thomas realized that if he was going to get any sleep before daybreak he had better do what he felt compelled to do, even though he thought the whole thing very strange. He got dressed and went out into the darkness. The moon lit up the narrow path into the woods as he walked along to the place he had felt impressed to go and stand. Then in a loud, clear voice he sang the hymn he felt he should sing. He felt a fool to put it mildly, standing there in the middle of the night singing one of his favourite hymns about Jesus his Saviour. But he sang with conviction about the God who was so dear to him. When he reached the end of the song he felt calm and tired, so he returned home and quickly fell asleep.

Sometimes he would think about this strange experience, but as the years passed he forgot about the episode. Then, one evening while visiting a strange town, he stepped into an evangelistic meeting. Part of the programme contained testimonies from various people who told about their experiences. A man stood up and said that many years before he had been through a great crisis and had decided one night to hang himself in the woods. When he arrived at the spot he had chosen he heard someone singing a wonderful song about Jesus, a Friend who can help us with our problems. The man had found new courage in that song and returned home. In the morning he found a minister who could help him. After the meeting Thomas talked to the man. The time and place were identical. At last Thomas understood why the Lord had wanted him to go out and sing in the night.

PRAYER: Lord, help me always to be led by you, to go on your errands, even if, at the time, I cannot understand your plan. May I be a blessing to someone today.

THE BLIND LADY

Therefore we do not lose heart. Though outwardly we are wasting away, yet inwardly we are being renewed day by day.
2 CORINTHIANS 4:16

Some months before I was to fly to Ghana to be a teacher at a mission school, I met another missionary who had worked there for several years. It was exciting to hear all about living and working with the people out there. Among other things he mentioned in passing was that one of the missionaries' wives was almost totally blind. But because he mentioned so many other interesting things at the same time I had soon forgotten this detail.

When I finally arrived at the school I found there were so many new things to experience and people to get to know. Everyone was so friendly. Arrangements had been made for me to live with the headmaster's family so that I didn't have to live alone. The family was from America and had lived and worked in West Africa for many years. It felt good to live with a family which had so much experience of life in the tropics. Both husband and wife were always willing to answer my many questions. They did all they could to make me feel comfortable and at home.

I had lived with them for over a month when someone again said something about a woman who was blind. This brought back to me what I had been told earlier and I wondered when I would meet this woman and how she could survive in a country where one always had to be on the look-out for snakes and scorpions and other unexpected things. Several more weeks passed but I never met her and soon forgot the matter again.

One evening when I sat down, as usual, to eat with the family the wife said to me, 'Is there a serving spoon in the dish of greens?' The dish was standing on the table right next to where she sat but she had asked me in all seriousness. I had lived in this home for more than six weeks without even noticing that it was my hostess who was almost totally blind! She knew her home and kitchen so well that she managed perfectly around the house. She also coped on the school grounds so it wasn't so strange that I hadn't noticed anything. She never spoke about her handicap and was one of the happiest people I have met. Yet she knew that soon she would be totally blind. That is why she had started to learn to read Braille and memorize all kinds of things which would be useful to have stored in her memory when she could no longer see.

I soon discovered the secret of her positive attitude to life. Every day she took plenty of time to be with God in prayer and Bible study. In this way she was strengthened from within to manage her outer difficulties.

PRAYER: Help me, Father, to realize that I need new strength from you every day, even when everything seems to be running smoothly.

SO PERFECTLY BEAUTIFUL

**A word aptly spoken is like apples of gold
in settings of silver.**
PROVERBS 25:11

In the seventeenth century there was a boy who loved to listen to beautiful music. When someone played a lovely piece Antonio's young heart filled with such joy that he found it hard to keep it to himself. A longing grew within him, a longing to play so beautifully that he would be able to give pleasure and encouragement to others. He had several brothers who were musical. They could sing well and play the violin. Antonio used to wish he could be like them. How wonderful to be able to spread sunshine and happiness to others by means of music.

However much he longed to have such talent it just didn't come. The only talent young Antonio seemed to have was wood carving. One day he felt so depressed that he decided to go to a famous maker of violins and ask for music lessons. Perhaps if he had a really good violin teacher he would be able to learn to play beautifully and fulfil his dreams. The violin maker knew Antonio and said, 'I will help you to make music.' He explained that people can make music in several different ways, not just by singing or playing. Antonio could, for example, build fine instruments for others.

Antonio agreed to learn to make violins from this craftsman and musician. He worked with him for many years. By the time Antonio was 60 years old there was not much he didn't know about string instruments. So he set about seriously trying to produce the perfect sound. He experimented with changes in the shape of the instrument, and in the end felt he had found a tone which was the most perfect he could achieve. Before he died at the age of 90 he had built over 1,000 wonderful instruments. They became known all over the world. Still today, 240 years after Antonio Stradivari's death, the instruments which he made are the most sought-after by musicians and collectors. Many other violin makers have spent many years trying to find the secret behind Stradivari's instruments. But it still remains a secret. No one has been able to copy his tone quality.

Antonio Stradivari had his dream of giving the world beautiful music fulfilled. Have you a similar longing? If so, use the talents you have — your voice, your kindly words, your smile, your thoughtfulness, your words of encouragement at just the right time. It's possible to spread joy and music in many different ways.

PRAYER: *Dear Lord, show me how I can bring joy to others today.*

COVENTRY

Jesus said, "Father, forgive them, for they do not know what they are doing."
LUKE 23:34

During the Second World War my parents lived near Coventry. This flourishing industrial town produced important technical products, especially during the war. It therefore became the target of enemy attacks. Nightly air raids started. Every time my parents had to go to Coventry there seemed to be less of the town still standing.

During the worst bombing raid in 1940 Coventry's beautiful old cathedral burst into flames. It burned all night and no one could get the blaze under control. When morning came people gathered round the burnt-out cathedral and grieved over the terrible destruction. All that was left of this great church was the old tower and parts of the outer walls. Everything else had either burnt or collapsed. When the heavy smoke gradually began to lift some of the spectators made their way into the cathedral shell in order to see if there was anything left to rescue. All they found were two half-burned beams which had been located high up in the roof. Now they were shorter and narrower and almost turned to charcoal. These two burnt beams were dragged to the front part of the church where the altar had once stood. The first beam was placed vertically and fixed into the ground. The second was added as a cross-piece. There, in front of what had once been the altar stood a rough dark and uneven cross — the symbol of Christ's love. Someone wrote on the stone floor in front of that simple cross, 'Father forgive.'

112   Now, many years after the war, a new cathedral stands beside

the church ruin. It was completed in 1962 but the old ruin was left standing just as it was. The new cathedral was built by people from many different countries, even by young people from the country which had bombed and destroyed the old cathedral. All who worked on the project wanted the new cathedral to be a symbol of peace, co-operation and fellowship in the Lord. Every day thousands of tourists come to see this new masterpiece of architecture which is so full of symbols it gives them much food for thought. Many of these tourists go into the old ruin to stand in front of that old rugged cross. Now the words 'Father forgive' are carved in the stone floor in front of the cross. I have seen many adults moved to tears as they stand there. To think that in the midst of all the hate and bitterness which a war conjures up there were those who could have such a forgiving attitude to the enemy, an attitude which Jesus himself had to those who crucified him.

PRAYER: Make me more willing, Father, to forgive others even if they purposely try to hurt me.

EQUALITY
"Believe in the Lord Jesus, and you will be saved."
ACTS 16:31

If you were trying to give every person in the world exactly the same chance to get a certain job, how would you set about finding a requirement which would be fair? To judge the matter on some form of basic education would not serve. Millions of people have never been to school. What about money then? If one didn't stipulate too high an amount would money be a fair measure? No. There are many people who have never even *seen* money, let alone owned any. These people either produce all they need for a living from their own plot of land supplemented by hunting, or they barter. A money test would be useless if everyone was to have a fair chance.

Perhaps everyone could be asked to achieve some sort of physical performance? But there would always be some folk who could not come up to the required standard — those who are too weak, the dying, the handicapped. Should it be required that people do something specific to show that they are worthy of the goal to which they are aspiring? Perhaps they could be asked to make something beautiful, to sacrifice an animal, make a pilgrimage to some holy place, or do something brave in a war or other crisis. Even something like this would mean that millions of people would never have a chance to reach the first stage of selection.

When God wanted to think up something which would make

it possible for *all* the people in the world to be saved from sin and everlasting death, while at the same time giving people the right to choose, he was forced to think of something which was totally fair. It had to be attainable by the poor and the rich, the learned and the illiterate, sportsmen and paraplegics. He found something which would give everyone the same chance — a simple thing — to believe in Jesus as their Saviour. To make sure that it was something which everyone could do if they wanted, he put into the heart of men, women and young people the ability to believe in God.

PRAYER: Thank you, Lord, for making it so simple for me to be saved. Give me a stronger faith in you.

LOVE IS STRONGER THAN WEAPONS

Love is . . . not self-seeking, it is not easily angered, it keeps no record of wrongs. . . . Love never fails.
1 CORINTHIANS 13:4, 5, 8

The Mickelson family had chosen to work as missionaries in an almost unknown area of Papua New Guinea. They were to try to make contact with a tribe living in a valley deep in the heart of the country. It was not a large tribe, consisting as it did of not more than 60,000 people. The only thing anyone knew for sure about the Danis was that they were very primitive, ill-tempered and dangerous. The government didn't dare send police or soldiers to that area. It was far too dangerous a place.

When the authorities found out that the Mickelson family were to go into the Dani area they made it clear to them that they entered the area at their own risk and that they should not expect any form of help in an emergency. But the Mickelsons believed they had a weapon which was stronger and more reliable than guns — love. They planned to challenge these hard and callous people with this weapon. They took nothing else with which to defend themselves.

On reaching the area they built themselves a little house and began to grow vegetables. They shared what they had grown with members of the tribe, they gave medicines to those who needed them, and took part in the ceremonies which the Danis thought were so important. They lived as one with the people, yet differently. They lived out their love to these primitive folk in a way which made a strong impression on the tribe. As time passed they were able to tell the Danis a little about Jesus. The Danis became more and more curious about these white people who behaved so differently. For the first time in their history they gained confidence in someone who was not of their tribe. They went further, and began to want to be like the Mickelson family. This does not mean that they all suddenly wanted to become Christians, but the area which had been so dangerous that even an army dare not go in, became a place that was safe enough to build a small airstrip. Now it was no longer risky to have contact with the Danis. They could be trusted. Love had achieved what weapons had failed to do.

PRAYER: O Lord, help me to use your weapon — love — in trying to win people for you.

SHE WANTED TO GIVE

"Sell your possessions and give to the poor. Provide purses for yourselves that will not wear out, a treasure in heaven that will not be exhausted, where no thief comes near. . . . For where your treasure is, there your heart will be also."
LUKE 12:33, 34

1839 was a problem year for George Müller. He faced constant financial difficulties. Where would the money come from to provide for the many children he had in his care in the several children's homes he had established? Where would the money come from to pay the wages of those he employed in the homes and in the schools? God was his only source of finance. Sometimes he would have enough in the kitty to last a week, sometimes for only three days. But he continued to rely on God. God honoured his trust by various means. Usually by influencing people to give.

By August 1839 the kitty was at a very low ebb. Müller was beginning to wonder why God did not do more and do so quickly! He had a real crisis on his hands, and if God did not do something soon many homeless children would be affected. At that point a woman came to Müller and gave him what in those days was a large sum of money, £82. She said it was for the children. George Müller knew her. She was not a wealthy woman. She had worked hard over the years and lived frugally. Hence she had been able to save and invest a little. It grew into quite a tidy sum of money. Enough, in fact, to retire on. But she had read the text you have just read today, and felt that God was speaking to her directly. She was of the opinion that one should not just believe but do what Jesus said. So that is what she did. She sold most of her possessions and gave the proceeds to the poor *before* her gift to Müller. She felt happy and was sure she had done the right thing. She could not see why she should have more than she needed when there were so many who did not even have enough to live on. This £82 was money she had got together by selling the last of her valuables. All she had now was a simple home and two capable hands with which she was determined to carry on working to earn her keep. The money came just in time to avert a real crisis in the economy of the children's home.

Nearly thirty years later Müller asked the lady, who was by then elderly, if she had ever regretted selling all she had and giving it to the poor. She looked him straight in the eyes and said that not for a moment had she wished it undone. Instead it had given her a lasting sense of peace and joy.

PRAYER: Lord, give me a measure of your grace to care for those around me who need help.

RICHEST IN THE WORLD

We know that we have passed from death to life, because
we love our brothers.
1 JOHN 3:14

At the age of 53 John D. Rockefeller senior was the richest man in the world. He had worked hard to amass so much money, and had not always taken his fellow men into account in his race for success. There were many people who felt very bitter towards him. However, his company and his investments were successful. Hence the fortune.

You would think that a man who was so rich that he could buy what he wanted, travel where he liked, and do exactly what he felt like doing would be a very happy man. But when Rockefeller was 53 he was ill and weak and anxious. The only thing he could eat was biscuits with milk. He could keep nothing else down. He had lost all his hair, even his eyebrows. It seemed as though he wouldn't have much longer to live. As he lay and thought about this during his long sleepless nights he gradually came to the realization that when he died he wouldn't be able to take a single cent with him.

What then was the point of having money? That was a question on which he worked hard to find an answer. And he found it. If you have money, you should share it with those who need help. This was not a new thought, you might say, but it was new to Rockefeller. He now began to invest more and more in medical research and other valuable help-projects. During what remained of his life he gave away 600 million dollars.

But what happened to Rockefeller himself — this sick, restless man? He was completely changed. First and foremost he began to feel much better now that he was thinking about others and not just about himself. His appetite came back. He found new joy in life. He even began to feel young again. Those who thought he only had a year left to live were amazed to see him grow stronger and healthier every day that passed. In fact his health improved so much that he lived to be 98 years old!

His life-style changed too. He was no longer a hated recluse. His interest in others made him realize true friends were won not bought. His thoughtfulness was very much appreciated and he felt great joy when he saw that his efforts and money made others happy and helped save lives. His change of attitude almost certainly saved him from an early death too.

PRAYER: Thank you for what you have given me in life, Lord. Help me to show my gratitude by sharing what I have with others.

WHO DOES THE STEERING?

For we are God's workmanship, created in Christ Jesus to do good works, which God prepared in advance for us to do.
EPHESIANS 2:10

In your home you probably have two instruments with very similar names: a thermostat and a thermometer. They are both used in connection with the temperature, but in different ways. The thermometer is a small glass tube with mercury in a small glass ball at the bottom. As the atmosphere warms up around the thermometer the mercury expands up the tube. On the graduated scale beside the tube you can read off how warm it is in the room. If you open the window on a cold day the level of the mercury sinks in the thermometer because when it gets colder it takes up less room. We have an outside thermometer near our kitchen window in Sweden so that we can see how cold it is outside and how much warm clothing we will need to put on before going out. A thermometer actually does only one thing. It shows what the temperature is around because it is influenced by its surroundings.

It is less easy to see how a thermostat works as its mechanism is usually enclosed. In order to work, it needs to be connected to the electricity supply. Inside the box there is a bimetallic strip which is made up of two bands of metal with different thermal expansions. This means that the strip of metal bends when only one side expands, thus triggering the mechanism to switch off the power so that the boiler, for example, turns off and the room gradually cools down. Then the metal strip straightens out again. When this happens the heater turns on once more, activated by the pressure from the now straight bimetallic strip. This ensure that the room stays at an even, preset temperature. The same thing happens with electric ovens and irons. You can adjust them to the exact heat you require and then the thermostat sees to it that this level is maintained.

In a way the thermostat reacts to the temperature just like a thermometer, but it does something more than that. Instead of merely allowing itself to be affected by the temperature around it, the thermostat sees to is that it affects its surroundings for the better.

PRAYER: Lord, you have created me to react to my surroundings in a way which brings joy and benefit. Let me not be influenced negatively by others around me.

THE BODY'S PURIFYING PLANT

Everyone who has this hope in him purifies himself,
just as he is pure.
1 JOHN 3:3

When you burn wood you notice that smoke is given off and ashes are left after the burning process. In every cell of your body something similar to burning or combustion takes place. This happens when the cells take up nutrients from the blood and, by means of a chemical reaction, burn up the food, changing most of it into energy. Even in these small cells rubbish collects in connection with the burning process. There are innumerable cells in your body and all of them give off waste products. When you consider this you realize that the body must have some form of purifying plant or you would soon become ill from all the toxic waste.

A person's purifying plant consists of two kidneys, each about 12cm long and 6cm wide, weighing about 150 grammes each. The job of the kidney is to act as a filter, taking out of the body fluids which are unhealthy. The kidney's main job is to see to it that the composition of the blood isn't altered. To filter the blood only once a day wouldn't be enough to keep us healthy. Blood plasma seeps through the kidneys day and night. Despite the fact that they are so small they can accomplish their task because of the millions of small blood vessels they contain. Over a twenty-four-hour period the kidneys can filter a total of 160-200 litres of body fluid. Not bad for such small organs!

In order to function each kidney is provided with over a million filters shaped like small funnels through which the blood plasma is pushed under pressure. The kidneys are programmed to know which substances the body retains and which must be removed. Because there are so many small filters to share the work, a kidney can manage to filter and clean 120ml of fluid a minute. Most of the body fluid is returned to the bloodstream and only a small part containing chemical waste products is siphoned off to the bladder from which it will be removed from the body.

PRAYER: Dear Father, thank you for my wonderful body, with its ability to keep itself clean. Thank you also, for providing a way whereby I can be clean and pure in the way I live — with your grace and your strength, new each day.

PARASITES

**For even when we were with you, we gave you this rule:
"If a man will not work, he shall not eat."**
2 THESSALONIANS 3:10.

There are some plants known as epiphytes which need a host plant to live on. In the tropics there are many beautiful orchids which grow high up in the tree canopy. These lovely flowering plants hold on to a branch or the tree trunk by the aid of thick white roots which spread out along the bark. The roots never actually grow into the bark and therefore do not in any way damage it. Orchids have green leaves and can, with sufficient sunlight, manufacture their own food by photosynthesis. Hence they are totally independent and self-supporting.

In England there is a plant which clings on to trees. Mistletoe grows on certain species of deciduous trees, especially apple trees, and we associate it mostly with Christmas. The Mistletoe is green all the year round and can, therefore, produce its own carbohydrates with the aid of the sun. However, it is totally dependent on the host tree for its water and certain salts and other nutritious substances which the tree takes up with the ground water. In order to connect to this supply the Mistletoe sends down roots into the actual tree. It then draws all its needs from the tree's sap. The Mistletoe is therefore classed as a half-parasite, making some of its own food and taking the rest from its host. If there is too much Mistletoe growing on a tree so much nourishment is lost that the tree eventually dies.

There are plants which are complete parasites. An example is the Large Dodder which can be found in the south of England. When the seed from this plant germinates it sends out a long green thread which has the ability to turn itself round while looking for a suitable plant to cling to. Once it finds one, usually a nettle or a hop, it begins to twine itself round the host plant. Until then it looks like an ordinary creeping plant. But it isn't. Once it has entwined itself thoroughly it sends out what look like small white roots. They are, in fact, suction organs which grow right into the host's food system. Once this process has begun the Dodder gets rid of the small root it had when it first germinated. From then on it lives its life free from any ground contact. In the end it sucks the life out of the host plant with the inevitable result that both host plant and Dodder die.

PRAYER: Help me to be less selfish, Lord, taking just what I want. Let me notice the needs of others and be willing to give too.

HOARDING FOOD

Whatever your hand finds to do, do it with all your might.
ECCLESIASTES 9:10

If you come across a thorn bush which has small mice, large butterflies or grasshoppers, even the odd small bird impaled on it, you have found the larder of a bird called the Butcher Bird or, to give it its proper name, the Red-backed Shrike, now a rare summer visitor to Britain. Some days are good hunting days. Then the Shrike catches more than he can eat. So he hangs up the rest on thorns and spikes to offset bad hunting ahead. Sometimes the Butcher Bird has several storage places. He will even stoop to using the barbs on a barbed wire fence for impaling his food stock. Occasionally he forgets where his larder is, but on the whole has a good memory and really does make use of his food deposits when hunting days are poor. These birds have a very strong territorial instinct and will not allow other birds to 'borrow' food from them.

Crested Tits are different. They like to live in flocks and survive best that way. This little Tit is found only in the north of Scotland where there are plenty of conifers. They also store food, not just for themselves but for the whole flock. During the summer and autumn they collect seeds from pine cones and small chrysalids from various insects they come across. They don't put their finds into some large hole in a tree. Squirrels and Woodpeckers would find the food if hidden there. No, the Crested Tit has a system which only this species uses. The Tit takes each chrysalis or seed, makes its own adhesive, and glues its booty into small cracks and crevices in the bark of trees. But this is not done in a haphazard fashion. The food is always glued to a specific part of the branch of conifers. Once the food is properly in place the Crested Tit covers it well by gluing some silvery tree moss over it, hiding it from all uninitiated seekers of food.

Once winter comes and the days are short and cold, the Crested Tit needs to be able to find food quickly otherwise it would die of cold. By using this well-organized system of hoarding food the birds can easily find a meal without too much loss of energy and heat. The rest of the day they can fluff up their feathers and sleep.

PRAYER: Lord, teach us to make better use of the opportunities you give us to learn and develop.

STOCK-TAKING

**So, if you think you are standing firm,
be careful that you don't fall!**
1 CORINTHIANS 10:12

In most shops there is a lot of extra activity at the end of the year. It's the time for stock-taking. Once this has been done the shop keeper knows how much he has actually sold and how much still remains on the shelves. He will also know whether he is making a profit or not, by ordering goods which the customer really wants to buy.

New Year's Eve is a good day on which to undertake some personal stock-taking.

Why not pause a while before the new year starts, and take a look at your spiritual life. Where do you stand? Have you taken time to know God better and understand his Word? Are you becoming more like him? If the answer is yes, you have a lot to thank God for. He gives spiritual growth to those who want it. If the answer is no, you can ask yourself several questions. For example, have you simply not wanted to grow closer to God, choosing rather to follow him at a distance, and only when it happened to suit you?

Back to the world of shopping for a moment. The owner of a shop can never be sure that his plans for the future will give good returns. Sometimes wrong decisions are made with the loss of large sums of money which have been invested in the company. But there is one thing you can do in your spiritual stock-taking which will bring you sure returns: invest your heart and life in God's company. You will not be disappointed. With him you will succeed beyond your best expectations. Another certainty is that however good the past year has been, the coming one will be even better. It all depends on your decision.

121

Before the new year begins go to God in prayer to make sure you are standing firm in him. As a result your stock-taking will yield a handsome profit.

PRAYER: Thank you, Lord, for all that you have done for me during the past year, and for all that you are so keen to do for me in the future. I give myself completely to you.

NEW YEAR'S EVE FIREWORKS

There will be terrible times in the last days. People will be lovers of themselves (and) lovers of money.
2 TIMOTHY 3:1, 2

For some time Eric had been looking forward to New Year's Eve. Not because it would be the beginning of a new year but because of the great firework display which was the custom on New Year's Eve in his country, Sweden. He had actually started to plan for this as far back as October, and all the money he could scrape together since then amounted to a tidy sum. With this he intended buying as many bangers and rockets as possible. There were only a few days left till New Year's Eve. On several occasions he had walked past the shop, looking at the prices and calculating how many he could afford.

No one in the family could avoid noticing Eric's interest in bangers and rockets. His family was the kind of Christian family who shared and gave away rather than spent money on selfish things. His parents didn't say much, but they were sorry to see that he didn't put more value on his money than to burn it up in a few minutes at midnight at the start of the new year. But they didn't want to interfere. It was his own money and he was old enough to do with it what he wished.

Eric's family had a special custom. They read a chapter from the Bible each morning in their own private worships. On the day Eric had planned to go to the shop he had been so preoccupied that he had forgotten to read his chapter for the day. He remembered, however, just as he was about to leave for the shop. He went up to his room. The chapter he read was the same one today's text is taken from. After reading through the chapter he put his Bible down and thought for a long time about the money he had saved. Would it be selfish of him to spend so much on something which had no lasting value? The more he thought about it the more sure he became. It didn't take him long to make a decision. He went to the shop and bought a small bag of the cheaper fireworks. He was going to have some fun, but the rest of his savings he was going to put to something more worth while.

PRAYER: Lord, you gave so much for us. Instil in us a spirit of generosity so that we may share what we have with others.

LY